"The main fact of life for me is love or its absence."

*"Feelings are both feel of, and feel for. . . .
Heartless sentience is sensuality, the feel of,
without feeling for."*

The Facts of Life

"A welcome departure from things clinical and psychological to things poetic and spiritual. Laing the psychoanalyst, is now Laing, the creative thinker."

—*London Free Press*

"Different and refreshing . . . a fascinating sequel to his
many other books."

—*Minneapolis Tribune*

THE
FACTS OF LIFE

R. D. Laing

BALLANTINE BOOKS • NEW YORK

Grateful acknowledgement is made to the following for permission to reprint previously published material:

American Psychiatric Association: 'Old and New Information about Electroshock' by Ugo Cerletti MD, from *American Journal of Psychiatry*, 107, pp. 87–94. Copyright © 1950 by the American Psychiatric Association.

Alfred A. Knopf, Inc.: Excerpts from pp. 15 and 85 of 'The Myth of the Birth of the Hero' from *The Myth of the Birth of the Hero and Other Writings* by Otto Rank, edited by Philip Freund. Copyright © 1959 by Alfred A. Knopf, Inc.

Library of Congress Catalog Card Number: 75–38852

ISBN 0–345–25761–8

This edition published by arrangement with Pantheon Books, a division of Random House, Inc., New York

Printed in Canada.

First Ballantine Books Edition: January 1978

For Jutta

Contents

Who knows
if life is not death,
and death life?

Euripides

Preface

The main fact of life for me is love or its absence. Whether life is worth living depends for me on whether there is love in life. Without a sense of it, or even the memory of an hallucination of it, I think I would lose heart completely. When one studies human biology, one will hardly ever come across the term or the concept and very little evidence of it. Here is a contradiction.

I detest much of the theory and practice of natural science and biology. There is a frustrated natural scientist in me, who has little else than scorn and contempt for embryologizing mythology, for softheadedness posing as tenderheartedness; for ungrateful and ungracious attacks on research to which millions of people, including the assailant, owe their healths and lives; for the threadbare cliques of obscurantist and obstructionist organicism.

Nevertheless feelings are facts too, and I record the fact that the passages which I've quoted from some scientists still make me quiver with rage (Masters), gasp with astonishment (Warren McCulloch), shake my head and purse my lips (William James), clamp my teeth together (Sperry), shudder (Cerletti), etc. What is done to unborn children, mothers and babies in childbirth, to people who lose their minds, *amazes me*. I know I'm not the only one and that this only goes to show how many savage, primitive, atavistic, archaic, wild, deviant, psychopathological undisciplined, stupid, untamed, unacculturated minds still remain to be weeded out by natural selection, facilitated by human and genetic engineering.

I know that there are many who feel the same as I do about much of what I've written, but that there are many who may find much of it scandalous and preposterous. I've tried to *describe,* even my justifications. I've tried to portray, to depict, to display feelings, memories, observations, speculations about our life cycle, life before birth and birth, suffering and the repression of suffering. Joy and love, sex and death are hardly mentioned, but are not forgotten.

> *Aunque sepa los caminos*
> *Yo nunca llegaré a Cordoba* *
>
> Lorca
>
> —R. D. LAING
> *London, 1975*

* Although I may know the roads, I will never arrive at Cordoba.

THE FACTS OF LIFE

Prologue

I was born at 17.15 hours on 7 October 1927, into a family that consisted of my mother and father, living in a small three-room flat on the south side of Glasgow. My father could not admit to anyone for several days that I was born.

My mother went into 'a decline.' A woman was brought in to nurse me who after six weeks turned out to be a drunken slut and another woman was brought in. She was a drunken slut as well. Then my mother took over. When I was ten months old, her mother and my mother's younger sister came to stay in our house, my mother's father having died sometime earlier, shortly before I was conceived, I surmise. Around the corner from us my father's father and my father's younger brother and younger sister lived together. His mother had died. My father was the oldest of two brothers and two sisters.

My mother was the second youngest of three sisters and two brothers. My father was the only one in his family to marry and, with one possible exception, the only one ever to commit sexual intercourse. I was the only grandchild on my father's side of the family, and the first of three cousins on my mother's side.

On my mother's side of the family, there were two older brothers and an older sister, then herself, and then a younger sister. One of her older brothers had gone off to Australia considerably before I was conceived, and there one cousin younger than me exists whom I've met only once; her older sister had one child, a boy three months younger than I. For my first four years I think he was the only child who ever entered our house, once or twice a year.

From as far back as I can remember, I tried to figure out what was going on between these people. If I believed one, I couldn't believe anyone else. Especially at the time when my mother, my mother's mother, and my mother's younger sister were all part of the same household—from ten months to eighteen months—I could not believe all of them, one of them, or none of them, entirely.

I was not allowed out alone until my first day at school. It was almost insufferably delightful. All those creatures like me to play with. And *girls* as well! When my cousin came with his mother, once or twice a year, we fought, as was expected of both of us. We 'went' around the corner once a year, at New Year's time, to see my father's father, and my father's younger brother and youngest sister came around to our house. My father's sister very occasionally came by, my father's brother once a month or so, my father's uncle once every three months or so, my father's father never. His visits ended sometime between my conception and birth.

My father regarded his father as having murdered his mother 'systematically' over the years. The last time he 'ever set foot in the door of our house' (according to my parents), the radio was on; he sat down and told my mother to turn it off. My father told my mother to do nothing of the kind. Old Pa, as my father's father was called, told my mother to turn it off. And so on. Eventually my father said, 'This is my house, and the radio will stay on unless I say so!' Old Pa said, 'Don't you speak to your father like that!' My father said, 'Get up and get out!' Old Pa reminded him once more whom he was speaking to. My father pointed out he knew very well whom he was speaking to, that was why he was telling him to get up and get out. Old Pa made no move, whereupon my father went to throw him out 'by the scruff of the neck.' The fight was on. Old Pa in his fifties, my father in his thirties. The fight went on all over the house. Eventually my father pinned Old Pa on his back across the bed, and smashed him across the face until blood was flowing. He then dragged him to the bathroom, rolled him into the bath, turned the cold water on him, heaved him out drenched with blood and water, dragged him to the door, kicked him out, and threw his cap after him. Then he stood at the window and waited to see how he would manage to stagger or crawl away. 'He held himself up very well,' Dad said. 'You've got to hand it to him.'

My father's younger brother, Uncle Jack, who my parents always said had gone daft with heat stroke in China during the First World War when he was seventeen, lived with Old Pa, and took Old Pa's side. For several years after the above incident, he'd come around to the house. He'd knock on the door. He'd be let in. Not a word would be spoken. He would take his cap off and his jacket, keeping on his vest; he never rolled up his sleeves. My mother would push the furniture to the side and get out of the room quickly. I went behind the curtains. Then he and Dad would go at it.

How many times did that fight take place? Each fight ended when Uncle Jack was down on the floor, couldn't get up, and called enough. My mother felt sorry for him; sometimes she would give him a cup of tea, and he would sometimes give me half a crown before he took himself off.

The other person who came to the house was Wee Johnny. He was my father's uncle though they were the same age, the son of my father's mother's mother's sister. Wee Johnny was a perfectly formed midget. He had a perfectly formed bowler hat and a perfectly formed three-piece suit, and perfectly made shirts and ties, and a watch chain, even a midget-sized umbrella, perfectly rolled. He worked as a clerk in a linoleum factory. He climbed a small ladder up to his perch there. When Old Pa really wanted to stir it up, he would say that the reason Wee Johnny was so wee was because his mother, my father's grandmother's sister, had been imbibing gin all the time that she was pregnant and when she was breastfeeding him. As a result, he almost drowned in gin before he was born, and imbibing more gin than milk after, he never grew, and that showed what that side of the family was like.

One of my father's sisters used to tell a story about her and Wee Johnny to gain our sympathy for her. She once, for the first and last time, took Wee Johnny for an outing in Edinburgh. As they were walking along Princes Street, she became so embarrassed to be seen with him; people would think she 'had something to do with' a midget. She started to walk faster, and faster. To keep up with her, he started to run, bowler hat, umbrella, and all. She broke into a sprint, he ran as fast as he could, but she got away and onto a train straight back to Glasgow, leaving him, as far as she was concerned, still running up and down Princes Street trying to find her.

I remember the word 'fuck' being used in our house only once, employed by myself, at age fifteen in some such expression as 'Who does he fuckin' well think he is.' I still had no idea to what the term referred. My mother was standing in front of one of those floral designed wallpapers when the word impinged on her. Her face drained ash white, she slumped against the wall and slithered slowly to the floor. My father was so aghast he forgot to hit me, but managed to say in a quivering voice, 'Never, never, never use that word in this house again!'

It wasn't until I was seventeen that I entered a house with a stair inside and its own front door. For years I harboured the ambition of living in a house that had a stair inside it. I went to a boy's grammar school where there were no girls. At the age of sixteen, I still had no idea about what we now call the facts of life. . .

1 / Primary Data

We embrance not only the absent, but those who have been, and those who *are not yet* [my italics].
—'Of Vanity' *

. . . whoever shall call to memory how many and many times he has been mistaken in his own judgement, is he not a great fool if he does not ever suspect it? . . . to learn that a man has said or done a foolish thing is nothing: a man must learn that he is nothing but a fool, a much more ample and important instruction.

—'Of Experience'

The advice to everyone, 'to know themselves', should be of important effect, since that god of wisdom and light caused it to be written on the front of his temple, as comprehending all he had to advise us. Plato says also, that prudence is no other thing than the execution of this ordinance; and Socrates minutely verifies it in Xenophon. The difficulties and obscurity are not discerned in any science but by those who get into it; for a certain degree of intelligence is required to be able to know that a man know not, and we must push against a door to know whether it be bolted against us or no: whence the Platonic subtlety springs, that 'neither they who know are to inquire, for as much as they know; nor they who do not know, for as

* Here and below from William Hazlitt (ed.), Charles Cotton (trans.), *Essays of Montaigne*, Navarre Society, London, 1903.

much as to inquire they must know what they inquire of.' So in this, 'of knowing a man's self', that every-man is seen so resolved and satisfied with himself, that everyman thinks himself sufficiently intelligent, signifies that everyone knows nothing about the matter; as Socrates gives Euthydemus to understand. I, who profess nothing else, therein find so infinite a depth and variety, that all the fruit I have reaped from my learning serves only to make me sensible how much I have to learn.

—'Of Experience'

Il y a des gens qui n'auraient jamais été amoureux, s'ils n'avaient jamais entendu parler de l'amour.
—La Rochefoucauld,
Maxim 136

(There are those who would never have loved, had they never heard speak of love.)

My parents and I lived in a three-room flat.

My mother and I slept in one room in separate beds, and my father slept in another room.

According to both of them, all sexual activity had ceased between them irrevocably before I was con-ceived.

My mother and father still swear they do not know how I was conceived.

But there is a birthmark on his right knee and one on mine. A fact against immaculate conception.

When I was nine, one Saturday afternoon when I was accompanying my mother while she was doing errands on Victoria Road I asked her:

RONALD   where do babies come from?
MUMMY   from heaven
RONALD   I know that. But how do they get here?

MUMMY   their mummy and daddy pray to God to send them one

RONALD   and how is one sent?

MUMMY   you'll learn that when you're older

RONALD   why can't you tell me now?

MUMMY   you're too young to learn that. You'll learn that when you grow up.

That was that.

When I was fifteen, a boy in my class (in an all-male grammar school in Glasgow) drew a picture on our classroom blackboard, during the lunch interval. It was a foetus inside a womb.

Someone had once drawn a vagina on the blackboard in another classroom, and one boy in our class had once even drawn a penis. Thus far dirty drawings had gone. But this was a quantum leap farther. This was not dirt. This was filth. There were a few really dirty boys known to be in the school, two even in our class. But for sheer filth, this boy was henceforth in a class by himself.

One morning when I was sixteen my mother told me my father would have a talk about the facts of life with me when he came home from work that day. So I was waiting for him. He was late. As soon as he came in they exchanged glances. After he had taken his coat off, he came in the room, and said:

'It's time to have a talk.
I think you had better leave us, Amelia.'

This was one of the few times I can remember him addressing my mother by her first name, and about the only time I can remember her dutifully and promptly complying. She left the room immediately.

We sat down.

DAD   about the facts of life . . .

ME   Dad, it's all right. I've learned about them at school. (What a relief)

(This was the first lie I had told for, as far as I can remember, over eight years.

I was terrified he would try to tell me. I didn't know what they were, but I did not want to hear them from him.

And by now I was so sorry for him I wanted to spare him the ordeal.)

DAD   O well, that's fine, that's fine. Is there anything you want to ask me?

ME   No Dad I don't think so.

DAD   Well, if you ever want to ask me anything, remember I'm your dad.

ME   I will. Thanks very much Dad.

He had given me a book to read a few weeks back.

DAD   Did you read the book? (A stern tract against 'Self-abuse'. I could not imagine what that was.)

ME   Yes yes I did   very good book   very sound very sound.

DAD   I've always led a clean life myself, Ronald, and I've never regretted it.

I hope you will lead a clean life.

ME   I'll do my best.

DAD   Your mother has never had anything to complain about on that score with me.

ME   (mutter)

DAD   I learned respect for women from *my* mother.

When I was sixteen, a three-page circular was distributed among the Christian boys in my school, of whom I was counted as one, by 'The Boss' (a Church of Scotland minister, who specialized in converting Glasgow grammar school boys when they were ripe for the Lord at puberty). It drew our attention to the fact that a number of Christian boys had started to take lessons in modern ballroom dancing, namely, slow waltz, quick step, and slow fox-trot.

It pointed out that in modern ballroom dancing, contrary to Scottish country dances, and other dances, the whole of the fronts of the bodies of the dancers, who were of opposite sex, came into contact, albeit through layers of clothing.

Specifically, the breasts of the female come into contact with the chest of the male, and the genital regions of both might be pressed against each other, or at least be jostled together on a dance floor.

Even if a Christian boy held his partner at some distance from him, on a dance floor it was not possible to ensure such contact did not occur, inadvertently.

Some Christian boys might argue that they were learning ballroom dancing as a social accomplishment. They had to consider what 'social accomplishment' might mean in Sodom and Gomorrah. In a god-fearing society one might speak of 'social accomplishments', but this world was condemned as evil, given over to the Prince of Darkness. Other Christian boys argued that it was for the exercise. We were reminded that there were other healthy ways of taking exercise.

We also had to consider what sort of girls and women went in for ballroom dancing. Would a modern dance hall be the place a Christian boy would go, expecting to meet a Christian girl?

No. If a boy was honest, he would have to admit that ballroom dancing was undertaken because of *sex*. Jesus Christ had died on the Cross for our sins, a fact that should not be forgotten for one moment. Could one, with a good conscience, dance a slow fox-trot, and remember, at the same time, the crucifixion?

The Boss said he would not condemn ballroom dancing outright. It was unnecessary. We should pray about it, and ask God for guidance. The Boss had no doubt what that guidance would be.

In the Sixth Form, I think some of the boys 'knew' or guessed, but I never heard the matter discussed, and I can remember only one conversation I had on the subject.

My closest friend at the time was eighteen, I was seventeen. We were both beginning to read Greek fairly fluently. We had both read chunks of Homer, Sophocles, Aeschylus, Plato . . .

He confided in me that his mother had just had a talk with him. She told him that he was going to have a baby brother or sister in about two weeks' time. He was flabbergasted.

His mother further indicated to him that the baby was *inside her stomach*.

Come to think of it, she was rather more stout, but it had never crossed his mind that there was a baby inside his mother's stomach (by stomach he meant abdomen—the common word for abdomen in these parts was stomach, the same word as for the organ of that name).

I did not venture to inquire if he had asked or had been told how the baby got there, but my assumption was (and it is still my surmise) that he had no *idea* whatever how he or she got there.

No one ever told me 'the facts of life'.

I looked up the sections under Sex and Reproduction in the Encyclopaedia Britannica in my local public library, but the most relevant pages were actually worn away, and where not, so faded and smudged as to be illegible.

I dared not ask the librarian. It took all my courage to consult these pages in the reference section without being caught.

What if one of my teachers had come in? Or one of the boys at school? and looked over my shoulder at what I was reading! Or just asked me, 'What are you looking up?'

I looked through the biggest respectable bookshop in town, Smiths on St Vincent Street, but could find nothing. Eventually I went to the book section of the largest most anonymous department store, found a book on the dangers of venereal disease, with explicit illustrations—I had now established, just before my sixteenth birthday, that men put their penises into a thing called a vagina, which women have but men do not have. Then they 'ejaculate', which results in something coming out of the penis, called semen, and this goes right inside the woman's body. This semen contains sperm, so small they cannot be seen and one of them . . .

2 | Speculation

I was twelve before I discovered I had not been the first child to ask these age-old questions. What a consolation that was!

When did 'I' begin? When do 'I' end?
What am I? Am I?

By what criteria shall I answer these questions?
By what criteria shall I scrutinize these questions,
to decide whether or not they are answerable?

For as long as I can remember I was trying to figure out how I got here, what was I doing here, why was I here, why were other people here.

I questioned the here, when, and what we were in. But my own most immediate, urgent concern was what I and we *were*. What are we *supposed* to be doing here? Where is here? Did I come from anywhere? Am I going to anywhere?

Are there people who know more about these
matters than I?

Are we all essentially, equally ignorant?
but some are more ignorant than others, ignorant
of their ignorance, hence thinking they know?

Is there any *sense* in wondering
who or what I am and why I am here?

Did I begin before or after, or at, the conception
of the first cell of me?
Shall I end before or after, or at, my death?

Am I dead or alive? Am I asleep or awake? How can
I be certain this is not a dream? How do I know
whether my world is not a five-channel synchronized
hallucination?

I don't think I ever thought
I was the I that thinks it's me

When it disappears
the I that sees
I am no longer here nor there
is an I
I cannot see
but only be

My Face

I see it in the mirror
I take the mirror image, turning it round, and
place it in the space where it is now suspended,
between 'me', and the paper I am writing upon.

I take off this visual mask, an inverted reversed
image of a reflection.

What is my face now?

There are different kinds of 'feelings' in the
space where the mask was.

The more I concentrate on them the more porous
they become—they fade and dissolve into
finer and finer dust.

I thought I had a face.

We look into a brain, we do not see the sky,
we see only brain.

Looking at my head in a mirror I infer that if I
opened up my skull there I would see a brain.

I believe if my visual cortex were destroyed
my visual world would disappear
if different parts of my brain were destroyed
I would lose my senses of sound, taste, touch, smell,
sight
and all the other known powers of my mind.

Does this mean that 'I' would not be able to propel
the vehicle of my body because it was so damaged I
could no longer use it?

If it did not seem to be the case, how could I
begin to imagine that this universe is the
experience of this collection of grizzle, tendons,
blood, bone, neural tissue, etc., this colony
of billions of cells, all
the descendants of one cell?

The first cell of me carried within it all the resources
needed to become, given the precise environment I
actually have had, precisely what I actually now am.

What an extraordinary arrangement to be?

We would think it were impossible, but for the
fact that it seems to be.

I am the outcome of the way my genetic system,
carried in one cell, has reacted, given the environment
it and its descendants, whom I often call me, have
encountered.
The fact that I am writing this, thinking these

thoughts, is the outcome of this interplay from the very first cell of me.

Physically, my body appears to be a physical system of certain ways of its own, a part of the physical world, the domain of physics. What is the domain of physics? The physical world. What *is* the physical world? Opinions differ greatly on this among physicists.

It is very difficult, perhaps in principle impossible, for us to *define* the physical world, to set its limits and limitations, since our brains, without which such speculations, I suppose, are impossible, are themselves elements, I take it, of the physical world.

My brain infers from this world it senses, that it is all, including itself, a transform *into* phenomena *of* physical events occurring *in* itself.

These physical events occurring in my visual cortex are completely unseen by me, while I am seeing what I am seeing. Nor do they *look* like what 'I' am seeing. Yet without them, I would see nothing.

The physical transforms in our bodies, in and from the eye through further transforms in and through nerves and synapses to further transforms in the brain, seem to be the *sine qua non* of vision. Yet they do not appear to resemble the world: or even distal objects out there. What are we seeing? We cannot be sure we are seeing what we *suppose* is out there, whatever we suppose. Nor can we be sure even that we see some sort of copy, or picture, of what we suppose is out there. If it comes to that, we cannot be certain that there *is* anything out there apart from what we see. Suppose the mind, a non-physical X, uses the brain as its instrument. When the brain is destroyed bit by bit the instrument is destroyed bit by bit.

I am told my brain is like a camera. It takes pictures. The world is the brain's three-dimensional movie made out of millions of stills per second.

But my brain is itself a part of the picture.
What is my brain a picture of?

My visual head is itself a very small part of my
visual world. Therefore my head is only a very small
part of what is in it.

All my inferences as to how my visual world comes
to be here, as transform of transforms of transforms
. . ., derive from the *last* of these inferred transforms,
namely, the visual world.

let Z = the phenomenal world
let A = non-phenomenal

All the transforms except the presumptive last one
are non-phenomenal, the distal stimulus (the first)
being the most remote.

Not until, at, or after the neural events subtending
vision (and all phenomena), does vision (and all phenomena) occur. The visual cortex is itself a visual
object. The visual cortex is itself a member of the class
of visual objects, which comprise the last transform.

Therefore the visual cortex as a visual object cannot
be used to account for its own visual existence since it
is itself an object of vision (a member of set Z).

This would be to suggest that a photograph of a
camera took the photograph.

What I see is an event that occurs when something
happens in my visual cortex. No intact optical system,
no sight. The optical system is a *conditio sine qua non*
of vision, as far as I infer. People without an intact
optical system are blind. And so for all organs of sense
and sensibility. A distal stimulus generates a pattern
of energy which is transmitted across a distance. These
energy transforms undergo further transforms into

transforms of neural energy and after many adventures of transforms of transforms of transforms along nerves across synaptic junctions, transforms occur in the visual cortex the outcome of which is my visual world.

Is my visual world in my head? Is my world in my head? The visual apparatus is destroyed: I am blind I can't take pictures any more?

If my physical frame dissolves, I can't live in this world any more, because this world is a transform: the brain is the transformer and is itself a transform.

When we look at a brain, how could we guess that the sky, earth, whole world is a transform of the physical processes that go on in it? But the brain is itself a transform of what?

There is the world of phenomena (Z). Without, I infer, a domain of non-phenomenal physical events (A → Y), the world of phenomena would not exist. At every point in every detail the world I am sure of is subtended by and *totally* at the mercy of what I can only infer.

The inference I am forced to make from the evidence, is that the evident (Z) is a manifestation of the unmanifest (A). Shall I call the physical world both manifest and unmanifest? Is the phenomenal world a transformation of the physical world? Or is there *no* physical world except the phenomenal? Do we banish from the physical world, even, the phenomenal world (all we are aware of) *and* infer only therefrom, that only the inferred world is physical?

The distal stimulus is not a phenomenon since it never happens in the visual cortex, hence, the distal stimulus of the phenomenal visual cortex itself, cannot be happening *in* the phenomenal visual cortex.

How can I be in my brain if the brain is part of the picture *of* me?

The actual me of whom the picture is a picture can hardly be *in* the picture. Surely *in* the picture can only be a *picture of* me.

Maybe the picture I have of myself is only the part of the picture that can be seen in itself. But I cannot see myself. This does not mean I am not part of the picture. But a picture of whom, of what, and who sees the picture?

If 'I' can be said to 'be' at all, I cannot be only a picture of nothing.

This collection of cells has the impression that it is I. This is a proposition I do not necessarily agree with.

It is generally thought by neuroscientists that the collection of cells called my body, especially that collection that makes up my central nervous system, receives input, processes it, and the *output* of this sensory processing is the phenomenal universe we live in.
Since everything we know, including ourselves, is part of the transform, we can never expect to know as transforms what we are transforms of.

Or maybe we are footprints. Michelangelo compared himself to God's footprint in the mud.

The brain is one of the set of phenomenal objects. How, as a member of the set we have to account for, can it be used to account for the set as a whole, and all members of the set, including itself?

3 / Nature and Nurture

I take it on the authority of biologists that, biologically speaking, we all have begun in the same way.

Namely, as one cell, somewhere in one of the uterine tubes, or in the womb of one's mother.

This one cell is the outcome of the union of two cells, one from one's mother, the ovum, and one from one's father, a sperm.

The advent of that one cell was the beginning of that collection of cells which without exception are the cellular descendants of that one cell. I, as I write this, biologically speaking am a collection of cells, all of which count one cell, forty-eight years ago, as our common ancestor.

Moreover, I am told that the first one of me, in dividing and dividing, had, at the moment of its conception, the same genetic structure (with a few exceptions) as every one of me has now.

This one cell is the cell all my cells are derived from, by a process of it dividing into two, each of these two dividing into a further two, and so on, and on.

However it's a moot point whether this precise knowledge of our microscopic origin and growth into the macroscopic domain changes or settles finally any of the basic philosophical problems attendant on the question 'Who am I?'

For as early as I remember I never took my self to *be* what people called me. That at least has remained crystal clear to me. That is, whatever, whoever I may be is not to be confused with the names people give *to* me, or how they *describe* me. I am not my name.

Who or what I am as far as they are concerned, is not necessarily, or thereby, *me*, as far as I am concerned.

I am presumably *what* they are describing, but not their description. I am the territory, what they say I am is their map of me.

And what I call myself to myself is, presumably, my map of me. What, or where, is the territory?

I accept, provisionally, as fact that my biological being will end with the dissolution, dispersal, destruction of this collection of cells as a coherent system.

These cells of me will keep going together perhaps a little longer. This present arrangement of cells does not seem to know consciously for how long but we have concluded that we are not going on forever in our present arrangement as a human body. We, it, I, they, will, as they say, die.

This collection of how many divisions of one cell is unable to find a satisfactory resolution to a number of aspects of its own attempts to analyse itself.

This collection is aware of communications from other collections. Some of these other collections are reported to have stated that we are indeed temporary arrangements, and that like all other arrangments, our sort dissolves. Some collections seem to feel that a sad thought, some are relieved.

Am 'I' no more or less than this collection? Shall I pass away when it passes away? How can I tell? Revelations and opinions differ. One man's revelation is another's anathema. There is no consensus. There is not even a consensus among collections similar to me, or mine, that we are alive. Some collections have concluded that they are dead. Some have concluded that we are ghosts, we die at conception, and will be conceived into life when we 'die'. Who can say? Who can say whether we are alive or dead?

We are physical systems who, by our own experience, are *sentient*. We feel.

Without the necessary physical arrangements there might be, for all I am aware of knowing, no consciousness either. How can I tell if there would be a me, even?

The physical arrangements which apparently subtend my consciousness and my world yield no consciousness of that world if they cannot function in very precise ways.

The continued existence of such functions seems to depend on appropriate physical environmental circumstances.

My sentience is not necessary to my immediate physical survival.

I can be physically alive, and yet be anaesthetic, heartless, insensible, and virtually mindless.

We seem to be like all other living physical systems.

We flourish under certain circumstances, and we wilt under others.

It seems then that a healthy human being possessed of motility would have a tropism for its optimizing environment.

It seems that we have a tendency in the *opposite* direction.

A tendency actually to *create*, and to live in by choice, minimizing environments, and to seek to normalize our environment at far short of optimum.*

G = the genetic system
E = its environment

Am I a product of G and E? Am I G?
G's immediate cellular environment is my body.
My body, except G, is non-G.

* For instance, when I was in Honolulu in 1973, there was an international conference on the environment convened and attended by 'environmentalist freaks', we heard, who are now arguing that everyone is entitled to 'superpure air'!

G is at present thought to remain almost un-changed by its expectable environment.

As G receives information from E, my body, G reacts as the necessity of its arrangements dictate, and E responds likewise, and so on, until G can find no further responses consonant with it and its cytoplasmic E associates continuing together in the form we call ourselves.

From the beginning (conception) to the end (death) of the life cycle is E

plus	or	minus in relation to G?
for	or	against G?
do I want more	or	less of it?
is E safe	or	dangerous?
does E *welcome* me	or	spurn me?
is it friendly	or	hostile?

The *first* environment of G *must be*
plus or minus to G
E *must* react to G, as G *must* react to E.

The ovum is washed away. No *unfertilized* ovum ever implants. Implantation is to be *adopted*.
The earth is my mother. My mother was my earth.
The *power* I had as *one* cell to affect my environment I shall never have again.

Does E welcome or reject G?
Does G come as friend or foe?

G reacts to physical fields in E that we are only beginning to glimpse.
G is exposed to all radiation effects, electromagnetic fields of local and cosmic physico-molecular-chemical energy forces. This is all our basic environmental matrix; if that changes just, to us, a very little, in some

directions, in no time we may be dead, or genetically wounded for life.

Our genetic system directs our response system to E. It must be the case that there are many types of E's at every stage of our life, whether as one cell or billions, but basically, they are plus or minus, for or against me.

The environment is registered from the very beginning of my life: by the first one of me. What happens to the first one or two of me may reverberate throughout all subsequent generations of our first cellular parents. That first one of us carries *all* my 'genetic' memories.

Our first experience of this universe occurs within a uterine tube in a female human body.

How many conceptions are desired?

How many of us are desired *only* for conception, but not to be adopted by implantation? How many of us might have been better to take no for an answer then?

How many never implant? How many abort spontaneously? How many are aborted? How many abortions fail? How many miscarriages fail?

Of those that come to birth, how many have been desired all the way, wholeheartedly from conception to birth, how many are born because

(i)   they were conceived unintentionally,

(ii)   or implanted despite attempts to prevent them

(iii)   attempts (mental and/or physical) at abortion failed,

(iv)   though abortion not attempted, mentally or physically, it was fervently prayed for, and the prayers went unanswered

(v)   abortion desired but attempts inhibited by guilt, shame, fear?

If the women who have answered me are to be believed, the *usual,* the statistical norm is to have been *unwanted.*

There were many fewer abortions in the years up to, say, 1965 than in the last few years.

It seems that although people were more careful to avoid misconceptions in those days, because abortions were more difficult to have and much more morally condemned, many of us must have been conceived against our parents' desires and hung on in a womb through perhaps both conscious and unconscious attempts to destroy us before or after implantation.

The difference between being welcome and unwelcome, between a welcoming environment and an unwelcoming environment, is all the difference in the world. Even to enter a room. The difference between being welcomed or not welcomed!

We cannot take the life cycle of the *wanted* as the statistical norm.

What sort of reception awaits each new arrival (zygote)? May yes or no from E at this stage (zygote) reverberate through all the generations of that first one of us all?

Can E *lie* at the beginning?

E influences G from the very beginning. It takes unusual influences to alter G itself, but G and non-G act, react all the time. Am I that interaction?

I suppose that all non-G in and around G does not necessarily *influence* G.

We only know whether or not the environment influences us by noticing we are influenced. If we do not notice we are being influenced, we cannot know we are.

We may still infer that some E may be of the order that its influence is to render us unaware of its influence, in inverse proportion to its influence, e.g. a toxic environment may render us *insensible* to its toxicity.

Are we re-creating around us an artificial environment which has a tendency to induce in us an unawareness of its noxious characteristics: an anaesthetizing noxious sublethal environment?

There are countless ways in which we can all be killed by our environments. Some of these ways, not directly perceived by us, we have or may yet develop instruments to detect.

We have no way of putting a credible limit on the ways we may be influenced for weal or woe, without being aware that we are being thus influenced, perhaps without even dreaming we are thus influenced.

Am I unaffected by anything? One cannot pluck a flower without disturbing a star, it has been said. And if the stars are disturbed?

4 / Feelings and Physics

In 1973 the question I was asked most often in the USA is *'How do we get in touch with our feelings?'* Is this state of affairs the outcome of the interplay of G and E?

Feelings, dreams even, may be cultured out, like the fairies, elves, goblins, water spirits, gods and goddesses, angels. G's response to certain environmental circumstances is, apparently, no-feeling.

Heartlessness and charity are manifested through a physical system, steered by or through G. Millions of people fear their feelings.

An American professor speaking of possible unconscious feelings: 'We'll try to catch them at the dream level and cut them off there.'

The couple, he a second-year engineering student, she a second-year humanities student, who asked: 'Should we try to get in touch with our feelings now, or wait until we graduate?'

Feelings are both feel *of*, and feel *for*. In either case feelings are now a commodity. Many people cannot afford the luxury. Heartless sentience is sensuality, the feel *of*, without feeling *for*. Experts teach how to feel either or both ways.

People have agonized over their feelings for a long time.

'I love and I hate, and I am on the rack' (*excrucior*), wrote Catullus.

and who or what can free a man 'From eager impetuous
loves; from vain and disappointing hopes; from lawless
and exorbitant appetites; from frothy and empty joy;
from dismal and presaging fears and anxious cares;
from inward heart burnings; from self-eating Envy;
from swelling Pride, and Ambition; from dull and
black Melancholy; from boiling Anger, and raging
Fury; from a gnawing, aiking Conscience; from Arbi-
trary Presumptions; from rigid Sourness, and Severity
of Spirit: for these make the Man that is not biass'd
and principled by Religion, inwardly to boil; to be Hot
with the Fervours of Hell. . .' *

But it's all right. The fires of Hell are now under
control. They are thermostatically regulated by chem-
icalization. Hell has been conquered by the industrial-
medical complex.†

ME   Can you put words to it?

SHE   It's everything. It's nothing. It's death.
             The mechanical death of human beings.
             A black hole. Zero.

A mechanical man has a pump, a heartless pump.
If the heart is a pump, show me a pump with a heart?
I am told that 'Thought' is represented in Egyptian
hieroglyphics by the image of the heart.

We feel E, and we feel toward E. How I feel toward
E is affected by how E feels. If I cannot feel E, I may
hate E or E hates me and I hate E. What's the point
of feelings anyway? Would we not be better off without
them? Are feelings being cultured out? Have they a
survival value?

* Benjamin Whichcote, *Select Sermons* . . . , London, 1698,
p. 17, quoted by Margaret L. Wiley, *Creative Sceptics*, Allen
& Unwin, London, 1966.
† Ivan Illich, *Medical Nemesis*, Marion Boyars, London,
1976.

COLLEGE
PROFESSOR
My feelings are way down there, somewhere, I suppose, if they are anywhere. I
banished them years ago, they were not
worth it. I hated my feelings. I told them
to fuck off and they fucked off. I've never
heard from them since. I've not an ink-
ling how I feel about anything. I can
hardly remember what feelings are.

Does our contemporary environment preclude the
possibility of a healthy phenotype from a healthy geno-
type?

5 / Life before Birth

Stages in My Life

A	conception to implantation
B	implantation to birth
C	postnatal life

M_0	mother before conception
M_1	mother from conception to implantation
$M_{1 \cdot 1}$	mother from implantation to completion of birth
M_2	postnatal mother

One of our great tasks seems to be coming to the realization that $M_0 = M_1 = M_2$

Do we have a genetic mental map of our whole life cycle with its different phases—mental patterns which reflect biological forms and transforms?

It seems to me credible at least, that *all* our experience in our life cycle from cell one is absorbed and stored.

How that may happen, I do not know.

How can one cell generate the billions of billions of cells I now am?

We are impossible, but for the fact that we are.

When I *look* at embryological stages in my life cycle I experience what feel to me now to be sympathetic reverberations, vibrations in me now with how I now feel I felt then.

Photographs, illustrations, films of early embryological stages of our life cycle often move people very much.

If you were to die now,
and be reconceived tonight
which woman would you choose to spend the first nine months of your next lifetime inside of?

That many people feel similar, and often strong, *sympathetic vibrations* (resonances, reverberations) when they unguardedly allow themselves to imagine how they might have felt from conception to and through birth and early infancy is a *fact*.

But what does this mean? Is it possible for we cells to record experience *before* specifically neural tissue arises, and to reproduce in later phases of the life cycle transforms, or variations, of such first experiences?

May our prenatal experiental patterns function as templates for some of the patterns woven into the complex knit of postnatal design? Prenatal patterns mapped onto postnatal regions occasioning disturbances of normal postnatal function e.g.

womb	umbilical blood	foetus	placenta
↓	↓	↓	↓
skull	thoughts	mind	brain

A person feels like a foetus in the womb of his skull being fed by thoughts from his brain the skull is a womb he is inside (crucified, dead and buried), and a placental-breast from which he is sustained and poisoned by thoughts (blood, milk, food).

It is at least *conceivable* to me that myths, legends, stories, dreams, fantasies, and conduct *may* contain strong reverberations of our uterine experience.

If this were so, some such later affections could properly and appropriately be called *hysterical* (i.e. uterine).

Some myths fit better than others but enough do to make me consider seriously the possibility that conception to implantation, and subsequent prenatal adventures, are represented mythologically in postnatal imagery.

Mythology may be a key to our embryological experience.*

There are I suspect even *greater* varieties of prenatal experiences (and of more interest and greater moment, S. T. Coleridge remarked), than there are of postnatal experiences.

'The standard saga itself may be formulated according to the following outline:

The hero is the child of most distinguished
parents, usually the son of a king.

His origin is preceded by difficulties,
such as continence,
or prolonged barrenness,
or secret intercourse of the parents due to
external prohibition or obstacles.

---

* D. W. Winnicott, the distinguished psychoanalyst, made this suggestion several times to me while I was studying under him.

During or before the pregnancy,
there is a prophecy,
in the form of a dream or oracle,
cautioning against his birth,
and usually threatening danger to the father
(or his representative).

As a rule,
he is surrendered to the water, in a box.
He is then saved by animals,
or by lowly people (shepherds),
and is suckled by a female animal or by an
humble woman.

After he has grown up,
he finds his distinguished parents,
in a highly versatile fashion.

He takes his revenge on his father,
on the one hand,
and is acknowledged, on the other.

Finally he achieves rank and honors.' *

Sargon was brought forth   conceived in
     in a hidden place   uterine tube
His mother, the vestal,
     laid me in a vessel
       made of reeds   zona pellucida
closed my door with pitch
     and dropped me
     down into the river   in the uterine tube

* Otto Rank, *The Myth of the Birth of the Hero and Other Writings*, Alfred A. Knopf, New York, 1959, p. 85.

which did not drown me

the secretions of the uterine tube, which nourish, or famish, us in the first seven and a half days before implantation, as the case may be: called by embryologists 'uterine milk'

           The river carried
him to AKKI the water
carrier who lifted him up
in the kindness of his heart
He became his gardener

adoption by endometrium

early implantation
chorionic embryo

       and then king †

mature foetus

      Sargon was put in
a vessel made of reeds
the door closed with pitch
dropped me into the river
       then adopted

Moses was placed in an ark
of bulrushes daubed with
       slime and pitch
laid it in the flags by the
river's brink then adopted

   Karne had a large basket of rushes
    a lid placed thereon
      lined with wax
   floats on river waves
until adopted from the river

  † Rank, op. cit., p. 15.

and so on

In many myths,	
the hero	zygote
is put in a	
container of some kind	
a boat	zona pellucida
a box	
a sphere	
a casket	
into a river	uterine canal/tube/duct
or the sea	
lands on the shore	endometrium
is saved	little understood adoption
and nurtured by	of the blastocyst by the
animals or lowly people	uterine endometrium
prospers	and
becomes adopted by	grows into a foetus
the King and Queen of	in womb city
the city	
	until
leaves	birth
finds after many	and subsequent adventures
adventures	in correlating M_0 with
his real parents	M_1, M_2

He is now twenty-nine.

At age eighteen he falls in love (with girl No. 1)
He and his girl are as one
Something stirs in him
He feels imaginative, reflective, creative
It is very deep
She does not understand

He meets girls No. 2
She understands
He starts an affair with No. 2, but does not tell
    No. 1
He and No. 2 discuss how not to hurt No. 1
He leaves No. 1 for No. 2
for a while he feels empty
then he begins to feel something develop inside him
    again
it is very deep
No. 2 does not understand
he meets No. 3
No. 3 understands
he starts an affair with No. 3
he and No. 3 discuss how not to hurt No. 2
he leaves No. 2 for No. 3
nothing happens for a while
then something new begins to develop inside him
it is very deep
No. 3 is not able to comprehend
No. 4 does
he and No. 4 discuss how to break the news to No. 3
he leaves No. 3 for No. 4
he completes his first scientific paper
he feels empty
he begins to feel creative again
No. 4 does not understand
No. 5 does understand
he has an affair with No. 5
    but does not want to hurt No. 4
he knows so well how she must feel
he leaves No. 4 for No. 5

he is now in transit from No. 6 to No. 7

Reconstruction

His mother gave birth to a younger sister when he was
eighteen months old.

M_0 = M before his conception
M_1 = his mother between conception and birth
M_2 = his mother after his birth

---

1. he and his mother (M_1 M_2) are as one

he and his girl friend are as one

---

2. his mother becomes pregnant with sister

he starts to feel creative with deep thoughts/feelings

---

3. he does not understand what
        is going on inside mother

No. 1 does not understand what
        is going on inside him

---

4. his mother and father discuss how not to hurt him

he and girl No. 2 discuss how not to hurt girl No. 1
      girl No. 3 discuss how not to hurt girl No. 2
      girl No. 4 discuss how not to hurt girl No. 3

---

5. he feels his mother leaves him for his father

he leaves girl No. 1 for girl No. 2
      leaves girl No. 2 for girl No. 3

---

6. his mother gives birth to a baby sister

he produces a "paper"

He 'knows' what No. 1 is going through and going to go
through when he meets No. 2
because when he meets No. 2
    No. 2 = his father
    No. 1 = himself as a baby
he = his pregnant mother
        his
  scientific
      paper = the embryo inside his mother

but at the beginning
he (embryo) and girlfriend (M_1) are one
then girlfriend becomes him as baby
he becomes his mother (M_2)
the next girlfriend becomes his father

Some 'heterosexual' men marry in this sense their
fathers

        mother   father

        husband   wife

slip of the tongue:

A HUSBAND 'What am I doing, marrying your fucking
TO HIS WIFE father-in-law?'

What indeed!

The world is my womb, and my mother's womb was
my first world.

the *womb* is the first of the series
                of contexts
                   containers
                   whatever one is *in*
                   a room
                   a space
                   a time
                   a relationship
                   a mood

                   whatever is around
                   whoever * is felt as around
                   one's atmosphere
                   one's *circum*stances
                   one's environment
                   the world †

* A woman says: 'My father was *there* but he was never around.'

† 'As far as I can make out, there is never anything but womb . . . It is failure to recognize the world as womb which is the cause of our misery, in large part.' Henry Miller, 'The Enormous Womb', in *The Wisdom of the Heart*, New Directions Publishing Corp., New York, 1960, p. 94.

Blastula

Shelley's dome of many-coloured glass that stains the white radiance of eternity?

a geodesic dome	flying saucer
a sphere	sun-god
a balloon	football
the moon	golfball
a space capsule	

the zygote and blastula in the zona pellucida

zona pellucida	a box		
	a casket		
	an ark		
	a swan		
uterine tube	the water	the ocean	a river

journey along uterine tube to implantation in womb	time in ocean, or drifting down river, till picked up by animals or shepherds, in myths, birth
conception uterine journey	exposure to sea or river in a box or casket
implantation reception by uterine endometrium	adoption by animals, or lowly people

Before implantation, the secretions of the uterine tube may be calm or stormy (the invisible worm that flies in the night in the horrible storm), plentiful or a drought. One may spin, revolve, float, fly; be dashed against rocks; be washed ashore and be washed away again, before journey's end.

Before eventual definitive implantation there may be many adventures. This journey to implantation may form a template for subsequent patterns. Implantation may be mapped onto birth.

Implantation

Implantation may have been as wonderful or as horrific as birth, reverberating through our lives. It may be resonated by experiences of being sucked in, drawn in, pulled in, dragged down; of being rescued, revived, succoured, welcomed; of trying to get in, but being kept out; perishing through fatigue, exhaustion; feelings of being frantic, helpless, impotent, hopelessness of being excluded.

Images of quicksand, swamps; exposure (upon loss of zona pellucida): then, after all those possible storms, winds, risks of shipwreck, drowning; experiences of breaking up, going to pieces, adoption by the uterus (M_1) at long last.

The basic possibilities can be expressed in the standard four-cell matrix

uterus

blastula

A bed of crimson joy or a battleground? The original template for all reception, entering: pushing oneself in or being pulled in; battling one's way in or a reciprocal embrace of love.* Does one enjoy diving fearlessly into things, putting feelers out (villi, fingers); exploring, with love or hate, a loving or hating world?

To put my proposition succinctly: birth is implantation in reverse and the reception one receives from the postnatal world generates a sympathetic resonance in us of our first adoption by our prenatal world.

I feel I am clinging to crumbling rocks, liable to be swept away in the torrent: hanging on for dear life, trying to get a foothold, never seeming as though I can get *into* what I'm doing.

Always trying to get *in*. Everything glances off me. I feel in a whirl, as though I'm turning round and round faster and faster and I could whirl away forever.

I feel out of time. I seem to react to everything just a few milliseconds too late. It's what I do in these milliseconds.

Nothing to hang onto: nothing to get my teeth into.

first extensions into endometrium

* Freud, in *The Interpretation of Dreams, Standard Edition,* Hogarth Press, London, 1953, vol. V, p. 400, suggests that entry dreams are birth dreams in reverse. Jones, Rank, Fodor, and others follow him in this. If not reversed by interpretation, these dreams are, in manifest content, implantation dreams.

chorionic villi

↓

placental villi

↓

fingers   teeth   toes

↓   ↓   ↓

getting   into   it
getting into the nitty-gritty
becoming grounded
established
getting a grip
being rooted

Chorionic Fear

I feel like a sponge. A deep underwater creature like an anemone.

I'm sodden with terror, suffused with fear, a terrified sponge.

I'm helpless. I can't move. It's meaningless to get out of it by running away, talking or anything. I'm quivering inside and out.

A woman of thirty tells me of a dream.

a piece of gum is going down an escalator
the steps of which are not moving
to a garage

She had been keeping a dream book. She was struck by this dream, of over a year back, which she had forgotten, because it occurred, she subsequently calculated, three nights after she had conceived.

She had not '*dreamt*' she had conceived until she '*missed*' her next period.

But she now wondered whether this dream could in some way be a representation of a zygote (piece of gum) going along the uterine tube (escalator) to the uterus (garage)?

a woman has an abortion

she dreams a white horse bounds free
from the narrow window of a jail

She is twenty-eight. She is terrified of being sucked into, attracted to, fascinated by, the sea, the darkness, the underworld. Since a child she has had the feeling of being a changeling: more like a dolphin. She used to say, 'If I disappear, I will have gone back to the sea to the underworld.' She has an affinity to graveyards, death, whirlpools. Twice nearly drowned, to the point of nearly dying.

Experience of a man in his late twenties

One day, at home, he went up the stairs to the bathroom. He blacked out. He found himself hunched on the floor 'terror-stricken, as though in a terror-stricken box'.

I ask myself, is it possible that he travelled
along the uterine tube   stairs

in zona pellucida	box
and upon entering	
the uterine cavity	bathroom
a catastrophic	
experience occurred	blackout and
	terror-stricken
	in a terror-stricken box

occasioning his whole be-
ing to be terror-stricken,
which is still reverberating
through all the cells of his
body.

Miss B, age fifty

She floats, drifts, is carried along, often in a spin

but she can never find	
a home	never put down roots
or make a home	never be 'earthed'
or settle down	

He is thirty-four. He has this dream:

sliding along a road	uterine tube
near his birthplace	conception
he has an overcoat on	zona pellucida
it gets wetter	increase in secretion
	of 'uterine milk'
he comes to an L-shaped	come through tube into
room	uterus

he is about to go into a	
building like a theatre	impending implantation
he puts one finger into	first of 'villi'

the place where he goes in
to touch two hands
(fingers) of a clock
he sits on a throne in the
theatre   implanted
children come to him   beginning of exchange
with endometrial messen-
gers establishing embry-
there is a problem on how   onic-maternal communi-
to communicate   cation at implantation site

She is thirty

She can remember nothing except pain and terror.

she feels like a ball of fear   blastocyst anxiety
she feels like a round
sponge sodden with   chorionic anxiety
terror

in dreams
she sees herself like a   blastocyst before
globe spinning around   implantation

there is a Paisley pattern
on the surface

she is overtaken by a fear   pre-implantation
of (the globe) falling   anxiety
she tries desperately to
procrastinate

she fears she is going to be   fear of
buried alive   implantation

her mother and her fear
tell her she has to be buried

Miss K is a spinster. She lives alone. She is fifty-five.

She is permanently up in the air, in a whirl, dizzy,
unrooted, homeless, unembedded
She travels from an island where she lives, by ferry,
train, and tube, to large department stores and super-
markets.
She is continually 'sensing' things going on around.
She is permanently a blastula, governed by the lunar
cycle: a lunatic.

    perpetually travelling
          in tubes, ferries   uterine tubes
          trains,
      going to big stores   endometrium
   but never implanting?

He feels himself to be in the stratosphere.
He needs to *enter* the world.
He works as a tube train driver.

I noted the following when I was beginning this
book. As I got more into it, the feeling passed. When
I start to write I have to overcome an inner resistance
to doing so. It was not always like this. I used to
plunge into writing as often as I could and could never
do so enough. But now there is a trace of physical
nausea just before sitting down to write. I sometimes
pace up and down and shy away from sitting down.
I can almost feel the *neighing* in my nostrils.
Once I start I have a run for it. Sometimes for

two or three hours. I 'surface' from it, involuntarily.
Then I'm out of it. And have to make a cup of tea,
or eat a slice of bread, or go out and buy a pack of
cigarettes, and walk up and down, and then overcome
the pull back, the nausea, the shying away, the feeling
between sneezing, a running nose, and crying, and get
down to it once more. Anythig to do with implantation?

A businessman of thirty-six

I feel I'm hanging onto a cliff with my fingernails.
If I let go, I'll float off down the river. I'll be washed
away. I shall be completely mad.

A dream of a psychotherapist

She is walking with a very disturbed young man
who has been her patient for several years. The ground
is reddish, soft, wet, spongylike, sodden, sand, by the
seashore. There are sudden dips and pits on the surface. She is frightened of falling in one, or of David
sinking into the ground. Then she sees him, in a pit-
shaft, naked with an astronaut's head-dress, falling into
a lake

She is past thirty

She makes a superficial impression, but does not
seem to be able to go further. She cannot get *into* a
scene or a subject. She can't get into the nitty-gritty,
and on through to achievement.

He is a professor of linguistics, aged forty-three

He travels to a non-Western country, where he is unknown. He cannot contact anyone like himself. He does not go into the interior. He engages in dangerous local currency exchanges. He runs into danger of being killed, or expelled by local authorities. He contacts the higher authority of country 'behind' the local authority. They let him stay on. Then he leaves. He frequents burial grounds in these non-Western countries. His imagination is dominated by images of tunnels, potholes, dunes, of being buried alive

Are issues connected with implantation?

One can stop, in a certain sense at any stage
One can lose one's *continuity* at any stage
Then one's cut-off past is liable to keep on replaying itself, even taking over the life cycle.

Many people feel they have never been born
Others feel they have never been implanted
Others are *just* implanted, unreconciled, pining, mourning, crying for the moon, the ghost of themselves as blastula before burial in the womb.

'The life of the individual repeats the life of the species.' So in the womb the embryo passes through the image states of tens of thousands of antecedent years of its development. In this state it is not unreasonable to suppose that the developing foetus may be at best somewhat subject to the images of the mother, who may be trying desperately to get rid of it. Her communications to the sensitive image of the foetus must surely be somehow different from those of the mother who is welcoming the new life, with its developing image enshrined in her heart.*

And I would not rule out the possibility that the embryo may communicate to the mother.

She had a miscarriage two hours after awakening from this dream.

> she is wandering through Jerusalem
> all is in ruins and crumbling
> there is nothing to grip
> no house to enter

She wonders whether this may have been the dream of the embryo.

A dream of the night before a miscarriage in the morning, several hours later.

> She is in a sealed car at the centre of a cross-roads at dead of night. The traffic lights are not working: cars travelling back and forth, up and down, whizz by. She is in terror. She frantically tries to get out but can't.

This woman was convinced the dream was the embryo's.

WOMAN   she wanted to get out and got out.
          I don't blame her
ME   how do you know it was a her?
WOMAN   I just know it

* E. Graham Howe, *Cure or Heal*, Allen and Unwin, London, 1965, p. 110.

During the night (two months pregnant) she woke herself, several times, crying out in her sleep, 'I must get out. I want out. Let me out.'

In the morning, she had a spontaneous abortion, against all conscious intention.

The following is a commonplace event to psychiatrists.

a young person
takes to his/her room
discards his/her clothes
huddles up in what is commonly called a
'foetal position',
or adopts another position
which he/she may stay in for hours,
even days on end,
urinates and defecates without moving
the person loses interest in talking or
being spoken to
he gives indications of great disturbance if
'interrupted' by external stimuli

This type of behaviour almost irresistibly reminds those who see it of the unclothed foetus in a womb.

The person concerned will often openly say that that is how he or she feels.

It is not uncommon nowadays for me to hear people tell of their birth or of their uterine life, as memories they have never forgotten, or forgotten and remembered 'spontaneously', in the course of psychotherapy, a 'freak out', a psychedelic episode, or some form of primal or radical therapy.

Thousands of people in every walk of life, of both sexes, in all income groups, of all ages, claim to remember their birth and before, or to go through experiences, which seem to them to be *re*-experiences of, and transforms of, natal and prenatal experiences. For a long time, I was put off these stories, somewhat, by my sense of their antecedent improbability. But?

Let me restate the argument of the past few pages.

I have to report that many of my contemporaries *feel* that what has happened from their conception to and through birth has a relevance of some kind or other to them now as adults. These feeling patterns deserve serious attention. It does not seem to me to be, *a priori*, nonsense, or antecedently impossible, that prenatal patterns may be mapped onto natal and post-natal experience.

A stockbroker, aged forty

from time to time very
intensely, at other times
always, but less so he feels
exposed,
naked
raw
flayed   stripped of vernix caseosa
helpless
at the mercy of others
no strength
it feels to him
as if he were a newborn
baby
he has devised a procedure

that mitigates his torment
he covers himself
or has his wife cover him
in leather
covered in leather he feels
as though he is mummified
and has oil poured
between his skin and
leather
affording him one
of the most pleasant and
consoling 'feelings'—sen-
sations he knows

restoration of foetal or
newborn skin feeling
as yet unborn

I am not considering whether these analogues are
'right', if that is a sensible issue, but merely that they
are actual. All of them I have heard or read, as well
as made myself, before or after having heard or read
them.

May there be a placental-umbilical-uterine stage of
development preceding the breast-oral stage?

Could some babies be confused by the disappear-
ance of the cord and placenta?

Could cord and placenta sometimes take on phantom
limb-like phenomena in infancy and later life?

I am impressed by the fact that 'I' was once placenta,
umbilical cord, and foetus.

Many people seem to confuse the placenta with the
uterus. The placenta, amniotic sack, umbilical cord
(all the foetal 'membranes') are cellularily, biologically,
physically, *genetically*, *me*. All of *me* I left behind in
the womb, or was cut off from forever when my umbilical cord was cut.

Could we be haunted by our placenta, our intra-uterine twin, lover, rival, double?

Could the placenta be the original life giver, life sucker?

our first friend or our first persecutor or tormentor? *

the analogy between
soil   roots   trunk   tree

womb   placenta   cord   foetus
de facto exists because it is made

My daughter aged two and a half says to new
au pair girl

'Are you a Brenda?'
Brenda was the first au pair girl

It is as though
we say to the breast
are you a placenta?
To a relationship one is about to get *into*:
are you a good womb?

___

* Some but not all of the suggestions in this chapter have been put forward by Francis J. Mott in an extensive series of articles and monographs from the early thirties to the present. This, as yet, largely neglected corpus requires a separate study. I mention here only one of his books, wherein he himself gives a condensed summary of some of his work: *The Nature of the Self*, The Integration Publishing Co., London and New York, 1959. I came to these speculations independently of Mott, however.

the first of the series becomes the category name
of the series

foetus   cord   placenta in womb

       umbilical   umbilical
       arteries   vein

Adam   tree   Eve   in garden
      and serpent
fruit   tree   roots   soil
        trunk
     two-way flow
     give and take

St George   spear   dragon
                         cave
                   maiden

    two snakes   staff
      triple structure
       caduceus

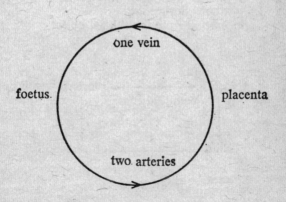

one vein

foetus   placenta

two arteries

faeces

foetus ←——→ placenta   { place of excretion
       food   { source of food

life ——→ death
death ←—— life

loss
renewal

giving   is it possible that the
receiving   *anlage* of these
                  patterns may begin
going   to be registered by
coming   our organism
                  before we are
going away   born?
returning

exports
imports

money
energy

the placenta —
      my other self
      my twin, sister, brother
      my incestuous lover
      my not-me me
        the pre-transitional object

foetus ←——————→ placenta-womb
          umbilical cord

 ↓   ↓   ↓

child ←——————→ breast-mother

         ↓

       incest bond

foetus·   cord   placenta   womb

self   connection   other   context

Grief for the Placenta and Cord

When I was eight I went one late winter afternoon with both my parents to see *Lost Horizon* with Ronald Colman.

When I came home, I ate a bowl of porridge.

The taste of the porridge seemed to merge with the death of the Princess from Shangri-La in the blizzard and snow as they are making their way across the mountains and the image of the young princess, ageing decades in seconds, crumbling, dissolving into a wizened old hag, and finally to dust.

Both felt closely akin to a very early 'impression', before words, before images.

Shangri-La   princess turns to old woman and crumbles to dust.

womb   placenta withers and dies.

One could remain in love with one's placenta the rest of one's life.

Could I have registered the ageing and dying of my intra-uterine lover, and could that impress have been reverberated by a configurational resonance?

6 / Birth

To be born is a momentous event in our life cycle. In recent years hundreds of thousands of people have been going through experiences as adults which they themselves feel to be related to their actual birth experience. Traces of the experience of being born seem to occur in dreams, myths, fantasies, physical events, or to be acted out in different ways.

The preference for unnatural childbirth practices, which seems to be spreading across the world, despite countermovements to tune into the natural process, has led birth, in many places, to be a major psychobiological disaster zone, in which almost everything is done the exact opposite way from how it would happen, if allowed to.

This is properly the subject of a separate book.*

She is twenty-six

she sits on the floor hunched
holding a cigarette in each hand
puffing in and out smoke from both through her mouth

* Frederick Leboyer, *Birth Without Violence*, Alfred A. Knopf, New York, 1975; Doris Haire, 'The Cultural Warping of Childbirth', *International Childbirth Education Association*, vol. II, no. 1.

mouth ———————— umbilical vein

hands ———————— a cigarette in each

umbilical arteries

a terror takes
over my whole body
a sense of *doom*
it feels like I'm going
to be chucked out
of the country
that my world
is going
to collapse
I'm going to be suffocated

then, she is
reduced to state of com-
plete helplessness
terror
her world feels it does
collapse
she is scattered
lost
no energy
almost dead
can just lie in bed and
sleep

projection into
the future
of
memory
from
past
viz., just before
uterine contractions

how it felt
just after birth

everything is all right, then
the world
it's going to kill me
crush me again and again
the terror is eating at me
it's like
being born = being minced
	= being eaten
	= being *munched* in a mouth
uterus	= mouth
uterine contractions feel like being munched in a mouth

The Compression Syndrome

the world is crushing me
the world is falling in on me
I * am crib'd, cabined, confined,
I have no room
no room to manoeuvre
no room to turn
I am suffocated
I am stifled
I am smothered
there is pressure from all sides,
	from all directions

it's a process of building up dreams,
constructing a world,
then BAM
it's all taken away
and I'm afraid I set it up that way for myself
I could provoke you or something, anything
just to flare up and kill me
so that I bring about my own destruction

	* The I's and me's in this section and elsewhere in the book
do not apply to the author unless it is explicitly indicated that
they do.

> uterine contractions ———→ terror

terror bears the *impress* of the
uterine contractions
so that terror itself is
becomes, as it were, the uterine contractions

present	past
I	foetus
live in	lived in a
terror	womb of terror
things seem to be all right	just before birth
it starts to crush me	
again and again	
I know I cannot stand	
any more of it	
I am completely helpless	
and exhausted and	
I lose all my money = blood	
I just want to lie in bed curled	
up, naked, under blankets be	
tube fed: not even bottle fed	

so *terror* now *behaves* like uterine contractions

uterine contractions persist as terror contractions

uterine contractions
being beaten   being chewed
being flayed alive   being minced
being crucified
being ground down

11 Nov. 1972   New York

After giving talk at Hunter College Auditorium, went
to a commune on 10th St, which was centred around
a small, frail, chain-smoking lady in her fifties.

She had been a psychotherapist for twelve years.

One day a man of twenty-four was in her office. He had run away from a mental hospital where he had been told (after his third suicide attempt) that he was an incurable psychotic, and if he did not have a lobotomy, he would have to be committed for the rest of his life, probably.

He had felt (he told me) all his life, stuck, as it were, in a manhole; he could not get in or out.

In her office two years ago he began to go into writhing, twisting movements (catatonic stereotyped movements supposedly).

It occurred to her that he was trying to be born.

He slithered from his chair to the floor, and she enacted with him his birth, playing the part of the midwife. It was over in about twenty minutes. He was delivered.
>He was out of the manhole, he felt,
>for the first time in his life.
>He felt completely different.
>No longer desperate, or frantic.
Subsequently he went through other 'birthings'.
>Now he has a girlfriend. Is working. Looks,
>moves, talks ordinarily.

He was the first. Now, Elizabeth has 'birthed' over a hundred people, both sexes, all ages; some, many times.

That evening, in front of forty to fifty people, in the presence of a camera team
>she 'birthed' seven people.
One of the cameramen had a go. I went through. A nineteen-year-old girl who was a Yoga teacher went through it; a fifty-four-year-old scholar.

One girl of sixteen had been diagnosed psychotic. She looked listless, eyes lustreless, skin flat, dry. She writhed, squirmed, contracted, agonized on the floor for about fifteen minutes until she felt she 'came out'.

The change in fifteen minutes was remarkable. Her eyes were bright, almost glistening. Her skin warm and moist. She said she realized, with wonder, a feeling she could not remember ever having before.

She had always felt touched,
but, until now, had never experienced *touching* —and had never realized until the sensation of *touching* arose, that it had been missing. Consequently, she said, she had always felt both fearful of contact, and a need to cling. Now, suddenly, this was gone.
I heard, two years later, she was still 'all right'.

This lady midwife came over to London in 1973, and spent a fortnight doing 'birthing' sessions, with people in the households and network in our scene in London. Many of them very disturbed; psychiatrists, therapists, patients. The most remarkable changes came over people in fifteen to twenty minutes. I saw her go through over twenty birthings one afternoon and evening.
I have told this story since in more detail to many psychiatrists, throughout the world.
What about the transference? What about suggestion? Merely symptomatic, surely, etc.
No one ever asked me how to get in touch with her. She is now dead.*

---

* Dr. Frank Lake in England has been taking people through detailed and much more prolonged birthing experiences. There are people all over the world engaged in similar practices. I leave it an open question here whether such adult experiences have anything literally to do with birth. My own experiences with intrauterine regression go back to 1951.

7 / Cutting the Umbilical Cord

White American woman, aged twenty-six, talking of her birth:

'I was a breech; but they turned me upside down, then dragged me out with forceps—I still feel the pain coming up on the right side . . .
. . . eventually I came out. I had had a helluva time of it, but could still actually smile.
Then they cut the cord.
That's when I knew the fuckers really meant business.'

the insult to injury

It seems to me possible that many of us are suffering lasting effects from our umbilical cords being cut too soon.

Is it necessary to cut them at all?

If one waits, it withers away 'of its own accord'. What's the harm in waiting? It has been suggested that we may lose 30 per cent of the blood we would have if our cord and placenta, together with the circulatory system connected with them in us, were allowed to phase itself out naturally. Since it *does* do so *naturally*, why interfere with the natural course of events?

If all is going well, there seems to be no risk involved to the life of mother or child in *not* clamping and cutting the cord, at least before it has stopped pulsating.

Under such happy circumstances, not cutting the cord does not seem to affect adversely the onset of breathing. I suspect that, in normal circumstances, breathing and the rhythm of the heart can be disturbed, perhaps for life, by clamping (throttling) the umbilical cord and then cutting it, while it and the placenta are still fully functionally *us* comparable to the guillotine?

strangulation?

the steady throb, the quiet beat
still echoes in the pulse of feet

scratch the wind
try being kind

too late too late
one can but hate

the two way flow
's no where to go

such perturbation
brings on transcendental meditation

that cringe
craves the syringe

When the cord is cut immediately after birth, there may be a response of the whole baby.

With others, I have observed the cord being cut on film. It is extremely difficult to tell what a newborn baby is responding to. This matter needs to be looked into further.

Could there be transmission of a very fast and global order mediated somehow from the sight of the cut, through the cord *to* neural tissue from non-neural tissue?

This presumably could happen somehow. How it might happen is totally unknown. However, if it is found to be a fact this will settle the question as to whether it can happen.

The issue as to whether it *does* happen can surely be settled very soon by direct observation, on those babies born in good enough shape to be reacting in a healthy way. This one issue alone impels us to admit that there must be a domain of ignorance stretching further than we can peer.

The question arises here, as in many comparable circumstances, of what we do in practice, in the absence of scientific evidence, one way or the other.

My vote is that the baby at birth is *feeling* it.

If we have indeed here an exquisitely alive and sentient being, like ourselves, even perhaps in a sense more so, might we not consider it logical that we would do our best to arrange the first extra-uterine environment into which we bring a newcomer, in such a way that would be most natural, most safe, most welcoming, most soft, gentle, tender, loving, human, non-disruptive, harmonious, pleasant to the sense of sight, pleasant to the sense of hearing, pleasant to the sense of smell, pleasant to the sense of taste, pleasant to our sense of pulse, posture, movement, timing instead of the isometric opposites of these common-sense desiderata in many of the most technologically advanced obstetric centres?

The way the whole birth process is shredded to pieces by technological interferences is a most remarkable feature of our time.

A man in his thirties went back to his homeland after some years. Going back, he felt more open, as though his navel was open and very vulnerable.

As he crosses the border *from* his homeland, away again, he feels a hardening, a knotting, a tightening and closing up again around the navel, and inside the navel.

what was once momentous
may shrivel to an apparently trivial memento

placenta   umbilical cord

yoyo   string

WOMAN   He said he wanted a divorce
         I had not expected it
         It was a body blow
         right here (pointing to navel)

After a lecture I gave on some aspects of birth,
including cutting the cord, a young doctor said to
me, with considerable intensity and urgency:
DOCTOR   but we have to break the flow
ME   but why?
DOCTOR   (stopped dead in his tracks, as it were—
          pause) Right. Right.
          but why do we do it then?
ME   it's just occurred to you for the first time,
          about five seconds ago . . .
          it's a very good question for us to ponder
          for some time

The response to
'What may it have been like then?'
reveals at least
(i) one's *present* projections onto our *past*,
    and may give an indication of
(ii) how we did experience the past.
How we now feel about a past that is beyond conscious recall does not necessarily tell us anything about
the *past* as it was then. It may only tell of our present
reactions, of our present responses, of our present
fantasies of then.
A woman says that she is now convinced that the
high temperature and feeling of being desperately ill

and going to die at a certain time of the year, always called the 'flu', is some physical memory of living through some intrauterine crisis when she was about three months old. For her 'flu' always comes on three months after her conception date.

Many people in the course of their therapy nowadays go through 'numbers' which feel to them, spontaneously, like again going over prenatal experiences, all the way back to conception. Some people go back to past lifetimes.*

* Stanislav Grof, *Realms of Human Unconscious*, Dutton, New York, 1976.

8 / Self-Description

The surgeon's hands cannot afford to tremble with compassion. The nurse's eyes must be dry. But if we are *au fait* with our feelings, we may restrain them at one time, and let them be unrestrained at others.

The more aware of our feelings, the more competent we are likely to be in restraining them when necessary, and the more easily will we loosen such restraint when circumstances no longer seem to require it.

Also in this way we will not need to use up any more energy than necessary.

The release of pent-up feelings almost always seems to be refreshing and energizing, so long as they do not explode into destructive conduct which we later have good reason to regret.

When I remember an incident in my life, I can recall it in two ways, from 'inside' or 'outside', as it were.

e.g. aged four

I am standing behind a closed door listening to my parents talking in the other room.

I can remember that situation from how I felt in it.

Or I can *see* myself standing behind the door.

As far as I remember, I did not *see* myself from the outside at the time.

There are many records of people who see themselves, or seem to see themselves, from outside themselves.

These are varieties of 'out-of-the-body' experiences,

which seem to me to be more common than many people suppose. How common no one knows.

It seems to come naturally to us to represent in a visualizable formula events we *feel*, but do not *see*, and have never *seen*.

If we want to *show* how we *feel*, we may, for instance if we *feel twisted*, represent this nonvisual pattern of feeling by a visual pattern of movement, or design.

The feeling of being central, of being *here*, may be represented by a dot we can see out *there*.

The first time I ever got completely pissed was in Crianlarach, on a Saturday night during a weekend in the hills, with the Glasgow University Mountaineering Club, as a first-year medical student.

I had imbibed quantities of rum, gin, whiskey, beer, and Guinness, and was now lying face down on a country road, about 11.00 pm in slush, snow, vomit, all under the stars.

Too far gone to turn over, or get up.

The world is turning. I am suspended from it. I ineffectually try to move my fingers with a view to clutching the ground, to prevent myself falling off.

Useless. I'm past it. When I shut my eyes I could be anywhere. In fact there is no 'I' to be found. Just whirling scattered elements.

Very very unpleasant; and strangely unstrange. Could I have felt that way before?

I had been resting my mind in a quiet place for days. Only consciousness and space as one. No I. No awareness of any object. The thought of a thought occurred. That very mere wisp, which ordinarily would have felt lighter than a piece of fluff, weighed an enormous weight, like a Magritte rock in the sky.

It was so heavy and an 'I' that had not been there before already was feeling heavy itself . . .

Did I weigh any more on the scales?

A consciousness can exist with or without a sense of an ego, an identity.

We are clear that the ego is a mental construction intimately chemically conditioned. It can dissolve completely, between two seconds of nitrous oxide, or any ego-dissolving drug.

Changes in the chemical environment of our brains change our minds.

Should people be allowed free access to the chemical controls of their minds?

Or should these chemical switches be under very stringent governmental controls throughout the world?

This is one of the very few matters where all governments seem to see eye to eye.

At 17.15 almost every day for several years, I feel like a drink (of wine, of whisky, of vodka). Sometimes I restrain myself. Sometimes I let myself have it. Why do I want it then? I often know *when* it is 17.15 by the feeling that comes over me. Why? Has it anything to do with the hour or my birth, 17.15? Or with my *idea* of the hour of my birth?

A late afternoon in February 1965

I am weary. Exhausted and dispirited. Fifteen years of study and research into 'wisdom, madness, and folly' have left me, it seems, none the wiser. Vanity of vanities.

I lay myself out on the floor of my consulting room at 21 Wimpole Street, stretched out on my back in the 'death' asana.

I shut my eyes. Drift off. As I do, I ask, with all my heart, if there is a power of healing, to give me some indication of its nature.

I am in a pleasant English country house. Large room, French windows. It is a gentle late summer afternoon. An older man, perhaps in his sixties, enters the room. He looks rather like one of those English scholars, who maybe once was a colonel, or something like that.

We have never met before but he does not seem a stranger. He suggests we go for a walk.

As we are walking, I become aware of the sun. It seems to draw nearer: to become larger and hotter. It becomes an all-encompassing fiery furnace. Until I am absorbed in and by it completely, reduced to one cinder.

I have returned to that dot again. Bindu? I am aware I can go beyond it. If I do, it could mean physical death. I am between life and death.

I find myself lying on the floor of my consulting room. I cannot move. I cannot lift my eyelids. I cannot move my eyeballs. I cannot lift a finger. Breathing is happening. I can hear the throb of my heart and blood.

I want to move now. I scan around my body to see if I can move anything. Eventually a muscle in my right cheek twitches. I feel a 'line'; very thin energy channel running down right side of face. I can just twang it; then the side of my mouth; then my tongue; then my right thumb; then I can open my eyes, and now I can roll over on the floor. I'm out of it. Back again. Time: thirty minutes.

I remember that cinder, that dot, that point.* When I was three I heard my father say to my mother: 'I'm going to beat him to an inch of his life this time.'

I knew I was in for it. He beat me. As he did, he began 'literally' to smash me to pieces. I knew there

---

* 'The natural soul of man is not larger than a single point; and upon these points the shape and character of the whole heaven, be it a hundred times as large as it is, is imprinted *potentialialer.*' Johann Kepler, quoted in W. Pauli, op. cit., p. 182.

was nothing more to be done. I contracted to a point. There no one could get me. On the other side of that point was . . . where I came from? After a while, I ventured out again. The coast was clear. The damage was not irreparable.

Cut-ups and Cut-offs

I awake and remember a dream. I remember that during the dream 'I' was 'in' the dream. I even believe I dreamt the dream. I, awake, do not feel quite the same as (i) the dreamer of the dream, or (ii) the I in the dream, as a dramatis persona. I am now the re-memberer and forgetter of the dreamed dream, the dreamed I. How have these cut-ups and cut-offs of me come about? How can it even be described?

In awakening there seem to be rapid positional shifts between

(i) I^1 who dreamt (actively) the dream (its author, choreographer, etc.)

(ii) I^2 who dreamt (passively) the dream (its audience)

(iii) I^3 who acted a part in the dream (actor)

(iv)   waking I^4 perhaps remembers a little or nothing of a dream, perhaps nothing of I^1, I^2, I^3.

However, from a theoretical position that I^4 may adopt, I^1, I^2, I^3, I^4 are all chips off the same block. And from a consciousness I^0, antecedent to I^1, I^2, I^3, and I^4, I^0, I^2, I^3 . . . $I^{n \div 1}$ are regarded as One. But am I single or multiple? Am I, indeed, at all? From my interrogation of my own experience I receive no unequivocal answer.

What happens whereby I^4 has lost its experiential connection with I^3, I^2, I^1, and I^0?

There may be cut-off points: these could be between I^0 and I^1, I^1 and I^2, I^2 and I^3, etc.

1969. About 8.00 pm after a long tiring day in my
office on Wimpole Street, walk out into London,
December. Turn right. Turn left. Turn right. Health
Food Shop on Baker Street. Jar of honey. Hail a taxi.
Home.

From Wimpole Street to Health Food Shop on Baker
Street is a walk of twenty minutes I would not have
made, if I had not wanted a taste of honey.

A taste of honey was worth more to me than twenty
minutes with Jutta and our child.

Moreover,

all of the millions of cells of me were moved, without 'conscious' awareness of endorsement, twenty minutes and one quarter of a mile besides where I thought
I wanted to go . . .

Is not this a serious state of affairs?

I am sitting in my chair, in my consulting room, listening to someone, in the late afternoon.

I reach out with my left hand for a glass of water
beside me.

As I lay my hand on the glass, I pause, and ask myself:

Why am I about to sip some water at this moment?

I'm not thirsty

I'm not dehydrated

Did I just hear something that gave a twinge I didn't
notice and . . .

no I don't think so

I feel relaxed

My mouth?

the taste in it is hardly noticeable,

It's not objectionable, now I focus on it

But my mouth is dry.

Strange it takes me so long to work out that, osten-
sibly at least, I seem to want to drink 'because' my
mouth is dry.

Why is it dry?

I don't know why it's dry. There's nothing wrong as far as I know with my salivary glands.

I try to salivate deliberately, without drinking, at will.

I can. To my surprise it is easy.

My mouth is now pleasantly moist.

I no longer want that drink.

A party at a friend's house.

He has invited several Indian musicians.

We sit on the floor, crowded, and begin to compose ourselves to listen, as they start to tune up.

There is a large dog on the floor near me.

As everyone becomes quiet, and as the music begins, stuff from the dog seems to be irritating my nasal passages. I have always had an allergic diathesis. I am in more and more difficulties, trying to stop sneezing. I desperately try to stop sneezing but it is useless. As the music begins to get under way, I have to get up and out, picking my way through, between, over, across fifty people densely packed on the floor.

Excuse me, excuse sorry ex- (sneeze) -cuse me sorry, etc., until out.

The dog and I had been close together in the room before the music began.

I didn't start to sneeze until the music began to get under way, and I realized it was not very good. In fact not good enough (for me) to sit there through it without squirming and cringing.

The sneezing got me out of it. But I delayed seeing this entirely clearly until it had served its purpose. I could blame it on a 'thing' I had, or something from the dog.

Only when I got out, I 'realized', I 'admitted' to myself, I had not been sneezing 'at' the dog, but 'at' the music.

I am sitting in my room. A young man is sitting facing me

I am filling my pipe
I begin to feel he is impatiently waiting for me to finish
I look at him. Actually he does not look impatient with
   me. He seems very much absorbed in his own misery
   I look at my feeling that he is impatient

The feeling, as I look at it, opens out to a memory
of me aged fifteen sitting in a chair, feeling impatient,
and feeling ashamed of feeling impatient, watching my
grannie (my mother's mother, over eighty), getting a
meal ready for me, after school, my mother having gone
to the hospital for an operation.

Thirty-two years ago,
   I was feeling impatient with my grannie
now
   I feel he feels impatient with me
she was preparing food for me
   I feel he feels I am preparing food for him
a clear example of a mild transient
'counter-transference' projection
   I attribute to him now, toward me,
   feelings I had had then toward grannie

As my awareness of the above opens out my feeling
that he is impatient with me fades into feeling impatient with him, briefly, and this feeling in turn
turns into a feeling if impatience with myself, again
briefly (a few seconds), to then fade out completely.

I am lying in the sun doing nothing.
I notice I am breathing in and out of my right nostril.
   When I try to breathe in or out of my left nostril I

am thwarted. It seems totally blocked. Is it blocked by a mechanical obstruction? If so, it must have arisen very quickly, within twenty-four hours, because I'm as sure as anything I was breathing freely through it at least as late as yesterday.

Are the air passages congested on the left side? but not on the right? The right side is completely free. I have no 'cold'. I am not aware of catarrh, or an allergic sinusitis, confined to the left side.

It is puzzling. It engages my attention. I become impatient and angry with whatever is going on. I try to push the breath out as hard as I can. I'm afraid I'll burst a blood vessel. I try as hard again to pull it in. To no avail.

I decide to pinpoint my mind. Let everything go, and then see what has happened. I do so. While my egoic consciousness is in abeyance, the left nostril begins to let air through perfectly freely. I revert to my usual egoic consciousness. After a few seconds it is blocked again.

I repeat the observation at least three times.
1) In a non-egoic pinpointed consciousness it is open.
2) In my egoic consciousness it is blocked.
The correlation seems clearly observed. But how is this effect being achieved?

The mental/physical operations subtending this trick are beyond the ken of my scrutiny. Unbeknown.

Why? And even, is why a proper question? intelligent question?

I've got a glimpse of what is happening. I don't know *how,* and I don't know *why.*

I start to talk to Jutta about my father, an old man, who has lost most of his memory, and is unlikely to live much longer.

I start to fumble with my hands, with my words, there is a welling up all through my body . . . a 'rush' of . . .

I suddenly become more acutely aware of everything.

I look away from her. I fix my eyes on a pattern on the floor to my right. It begins to go out of focus: my eyes fill with tears, they well up, run over, run down my face. My nose and sinuses become congested: shining clear fluid, thicker than tears, pours abundantly out of both nostrils and runs down my face.

I can't breathe through my nose.

An urgent ache appears in the back of my throat. All my respiratory system is being tossed around like a small boat in a very stormy sea.

My diaphragm, intercostal muscles, abdominal muscles, my tongue and facial muscles are heaving incoherently. If I try to control their juncture it will probably induce an attack of asthma. If I let it rip—

My face completely dissolves (when it used to be more brittle than it is now, I would have said it 'cracked up').

Fibrillations in both cheeks. Involuntary retraction of the lips, sobbing, and moaning, unrestrained for two or three minutes then over.

This sort of behaviour remains a mystery to me: incoherence, speechlessness, change of consciousness, unusual physical feelings, widespread disturbances of physiological function involving a global reaction through all sectors of the CNS, endocrine, muscular systems, etc., changes in respiratory and cardiovascular systems.

9 / Samples of Psychiatry

> If fire is lighted in water
> How is it to be extinguished?
>
> If the fear comes from the protector
> Who is there to protect you from this fear?
>
> —Nagarjuna, *The Tree of Wisdom,* verse 79 *

The first psychiatric 'clinical demonstration' I attended was in my fourth year as a medical student.

It was in a small amphitheatre in the Glasgow Western Infirmary. About two dozen medical students, including three or four female students, sat on the tiered benches and below us the consultant 'interviewed' several patients, all 'out' patients.

He asked them each their name, age, address, the composition of their families, had they any previous illnesses, and then inquired after their present complaint.

The first patient that afternoon was a thin, pale, bespectacled chap of seventeen, with marked acne. He had been referred to the psychiatric department by his general practitioner, to whom he had gone for treatment of his acne. But the GP believed in 'psychosomatic' medicine, which psychiatrists knew more about.

The consultant and patient had not met before.

* Translated by Major W. L. Campbell, C.I.E., Baptist Mission Press, Calcutta, 1919.

After two minutes during which he answered correctly the questions asked (all this information was already in a letter from his doctor; the point of the questions was not to provide us with the facts of life, age, etc., but to establish whether he was 'correctly orientated for time, place, and person' or not).

CONSULTANT	and what is your complaint, apart from your acne, which we can all see
PATIENT	I'm afraid people are looking at me in the street
CONSULTANT	you are afraid they know you masturbate
PATIENT	(His white face turned scarlet, and his red pimples went white) yes
CONSULTANT	how often do you masturbate?
PATIENT	two or three times a week

And so the interview went on for about fifteen minutes (longer than usual).

The patient was then dismissed, and a discussion ensued on this case for about five minutes before the next one was brought in.

I had never heard the word 'masturbate' used 'in public' before.

I cringed in terror at the prospect of the consultant asking us the questions he asked this patient, but he did not. He explained that masturbation used to be regarded as a cause for mental deterioration, but more advanced medical opinion now thought of it as not usually 'an etiological factor', but merely an early symptom of some conditions. He pointed out that the patient had answered all his questions dispassionately without a tremor in his face, and apart from the vascular changes in his facial blood vessels, no changes occurred in his outward behaviour.

In all but exceptional cases 'psychotherapy' was contraindicated as making patients 'worse'. There might be a 'spontaneous remission', or an 'arrest' in the 'process', or . . .

Dr MacKenzie at Stobhill had a way with involuntial melancholics.

When one of these Lowlands Presbyterian sixty-year-olds came in lamenting his certain and justly preor-dained damnation for his unredeemable deadly sins, with wringing of hands, groaning, loss of appetite, en-grossed in self-loathing at his own self-pity, constipated, having been brought into the hospital finally because no one could put up with him any longer, insufferable, his remedy was 10cc of turpentine injection into the but-tocks. This produced a raging fever, hopefully sterile (sterile pyrexia), and swollen burning buttocks, ex-quisitely painful.

'We'll give him a taste of what he thinks is coming to him (hell fire as adumbrated by fever, torture by the wracking pain, the delirium, etc.) and we'll see, when it dies down (after ten days), if he is not going to shut up and count his blessings.'

Nobody had been heard to come back for more.

100 per cent remission rate. 100 per cent discharge rate. 0 per cent relapse rate.

Clinical Conferences, 1970s

She is in the hospital because every time her hus-band, a travelling salesman, comes home she starts to vomit and continues to do so until he leaves.

She denies being sick of him

Is she *really* sick of him,
    can't admit it to herself
        denies the thought,
    but converted to a physical metaphor
        it expresses itself as
            an hysterical conversion symptom?

(genital sexual difficulties and early oral problems, no
doubt)

perhaps she is vomiting
        out umbilical blood via her mouth
        confusing him with her placenta?
perhaps she wants to vomit over him
        as revenge for his going away?
perhaps she wants to get her bad indigestible feelings
        out of her system. Which in a way she does by
        'converting' feelings to stomach contents, then
        getting rid of them by vomiting?
perhaps it is some transform of a . . . ?
perhaps it's some ectohormonal mismatch?
perhaps a birth trauma?
perhaps psychotherapy?
perhaps tranquillizers?
perhaps behaviour therapy?
perhaps an interview with the husband?
parhaps marital therapy?
perhaps a home visit by a social worker?
perhaps a physical examination of the woman by a
        physician?
perhaps testing by clinical psychologist?
perhaps group psychotherapy?

She gets very depressed before she starts vomiting
right   or before he comes home
right
right   well how about a few bangs with the box before
he comes home or before she starts vomiting, it might
break the coupling and the periodicity . . .
maybe   we'll think about it

USA

Man of 24: catatonic schizophrenic about to be dis-
charged, remitted after eight months, electric shocks,
tranquillizers, psychotherapy

PATIENT   when I came back from Vietnam, it was
(to me)   too confusing. Too complex. I had to try
               to figure it out. I had to get rid of all the
               lumber. So I finally made no movements
               at all. They carted me here. And started
               doing me in. I realized that I couldn't
               simplify my life this way, so I started to
               move normally again, and talk normally
               so they've reduced the tranquillizers and
               stopped the electric shocks and I believe
               they are going to let me leave shortly

PATIENT'S   but John I thought you were really cured
PSYCHO-   and now I hear you have just been putting
THERAPIST   on a show to get out. John, I am disap-
               pointed in you.

UK

father and mother
two daughters
    one thirteen
    the other twelve Anne
the younger one is the problem
    she is always running away from home
    she does not apply herself to her schoolwork
    she is untidy
    she is sloppy
in fact her mother can't bear even to look at her
    she did not want another baby so soon after the
    first
    she wanted a boy, if it had to be something

    since she had Anne
    she has become fat,
    lost her looks,
    her husband no longer finds her attractive

she hates her
and resents her
she often beats her up
Anne cannot do a thing right

Anne is in psychotherapy? Schizophrenic
there seems nothing the matter with Anne
she runs away because her mother whips her
her mother whips her for running away

will her mother have her revenge
by driving her crazy
or is it possible
that her mother might *repent* and *relent?*

forgive,
and possibly be forgiven

forgive us our trespasses,
as we forgive them their trespass against us

He is twenty-four. He has been having an electroshock
every three weeks because
the effect of the electric shock wears off after ten
days and then
he keeps going into deep thought
to do this he has to go into a room
he must not be interrupted
he has to concentrate with a total effort
he cannot afford to complicate matters
by making a single movement
by uttering a single word
he stays awake as much as possible because the
process is interrupted by sleep

he is uninterested in eating
he takes off his clothes
he pisses and shits where he is standing, or sitting,
of lying, immobile

as he gets deeper
he feels he gets closer
tremendous pressure begins to come upon him from
all around
it is like being born, he says

every time it is stopped, compulsively, by electric
shocks
he has to start from the beginning again

There is not *one* psychiatric installation known to
me in the UK, and perhaps two or three in the USA
where he would be 'allowed', or even 'helped', to go
'through' what he feels impelled to go into.

There is no place known to me where a young or
old psychiatrist may, as a matter of pure research
interest, be allowed to observe the natural history of
this process,
could he be trying to go through a birth
experience?
Is it possible that in an appropriate environment,
and with skilled therapists as accoucheurs, he might
be 'delivered'?
Could his actual 'symptoms', if one could be on
the 'right' side of them, be the channel through which
he might find release from his agony?
As it is,
he says he will kill himself if he is not allowed to
go 'into' his deep thoughts.
a further indication for more electric shocks
Moreover, the psychiatrists now feel he has become
'addicted' to electric shocks,

since he keeps on forcing them to administer them and some ways and means have to be found to 'wean' him off them. Perhaps brain surgery before it is too late.

A little bit of his brain cut off from the rest now may save more having to be cut off later.

A psychiatrist regrets to me that there had not been ECT at the time of Shakespeare, for then *King Lear* would never have needed to have been written; he would have had ECT.

A frantic looking woman asked: 'If I do not feel I exist, why should I not kill myself?'

'A trivial philosophical question,' replied the chairman of her department of philosophy.

USA

They met in Austria, her home. Moved to Australia, where neither had ever been. Then he was sent to South America. And now they live somewhere in Northeastern America.

He is away all day
She knows no one
One day when he comes home she tells him she feels like screaming. He phones the doctor. He gives her an injection. He calls an ambulance. She is taken to a sanatorium. She feels like screaming. She is put on a régime of tranquillizers—she feels even more like screaming—and electric shocks. She starts to feel like screaming again after the immediate concussion of electric shocks wears off.

She is put on psychotherapy. Electric shocks discontinued, tranquillizers retained and reduced, plus a few other things.

She came in three months ago
She is still in

She still feels like screaming
She has never screamed

USA

Her father is a hefty construction worker
Her mother is made to the same proportions
Her two big brothers are cops

She is fourteen
and has been in a mental home for three
months, diagnosed as schizophrenic

She has been subject to many physical and
psychological investigations
She has a one-to-one psychotherapist
She attends group therapy
She attends occupational therapy
Her mother is seen by a social worker
The father and mother have seen one of the
psychiatrists several times
Her mother gets pills from her general
practitioner
There is a psychiatrist in charge of her in the
hospital
There is a psychiatrist in charge of her out of
the hospital

There is a consensus among all family members that
she was sent to the hospital for the following reasons:

She sat in her room   while she should have
and stared at the wall   been downstairs with the
                             rest of the family watching
                             television

She starved herself	She picked from the fridge and drank two pints of milk a day, but refused to eat 'meals' cooked by her mother
She was half the weight she should be	She seemed rather skinny; the rest of the family seemed twice the weight they should be
She washed her hands and face in cold water	instead of hot water like everyone else
She wanted to go out of the house if she couldn't stare at the wall	It was a family, they said, of 'hollerers'; everyone wanted to be the boss. The streets were not safe for her
She couldn't stand the shouting and the noise and found she could get away from it by staring at a wall	Her mother felt that by doing so, she might 'slip away' from her
She felt she was made fun of at school because she was skinny	She actually was. But they did not want to upset her by admitting she was right
She wanted to stay on at school	They felt it would be kinder to her if they took her away from school

I am sure that I have stared at walls for many more hours than this girl.

In some circles this is called meditation—a way of resting, calming, emptying, tranquillizing the mind. It seems to me one of the natural functions, like sleeping, dreaming, waking, being interested in things. Like breathing in and breathing out, systole and diastole, open and close.

She couldn't stand the noise—neither would I,
                              I expect
   she couldn't go out in the street
 · she couldn't concentrate on her homework
                              very difficult

She had come across a normal natural resource, cultured out of her subculture.

There may have been a competent meditation teacher (someone who has spent years and *years* staring at a wall, or nothing in particular) in town . . .

However, instead of this being viewed as a possible avenue of temporary escape (the best action in some situations is to escape—this is not escap-ism), and a refuge (desperately and justifiably needed), this is regarded as the prime symptom of a schizophrenic illness.

Her family are not sent off to an installation of the medical-industrial complex in order to be reserviced so as not to spend their time watching television.

I am told 'the average Canadian' watches television for five hours a day.

Would they be any the worse for staring at a blank wall for five hours a day, I wonder?

But moreover (to be fair), 'she is a case of day-night reversal'. This is another ominous symptom of mental disorder and has to be stopped. She is awake at night when it is quiet and tries to get away from the fighting and bawling when the rest of the family is awake and 'at it'.

The point is that she is 'out of control'. Her social programming is breaking down, it might never even have 'taken'. She might have some genetic defect that

renders her more difficult to be socialized than her
brothers, the cops, for instance.

She does not eat what is cooked for her or at the
right time.

She does not sleep when she should, when it is normal for a girl of her age to sleep, when all the other
girls in her class are asleep.

She does not wash her hands and face
in hot water, like everyone else,
does this not show signs of negativism,
of *asocial,* if not *anti*-social conduct.
She does not speak when spoken to, sometimes.
She is sometimes in tears
because she is teased at
school for being skinny.
Does this not show signs of social
maladaption: even social manipulation,
suggesting an hysterical
psychopathology, rather than a
schizophrenic?

Her mother is desperately worried
about her, slipping away from her,
not getting her proper food,
not getting her proper sleep,
and the social shame (it must be admitted) of her
daughter becoming the laughing stock

but the *girl* is not worried she does not see why her mother should be worried	she shows no insight de- spite her selfish tears, she seems to be lacking in some, it is difficult to put one's finger on it precisely, but you *must* know what I mean, some lack of affect, of feeling; indifference, or worse, more suggestive of schizo- phrenia than hysteria, although we need not draw rigid lines.

just looking at her
she looks very healthy,
her skin is the only one of
the family that is not
thick, sallow, and greasy

schizophrenics may 'look'
healthier, physically, than
normal, and often *are*
more resistant to infec-
tions, some say

her eyes are bright and
alive instead of being can-
celled like everyone else's
in fact she is rather fidgety

possibly hypomanic
elements or

a trace of catatonic even
hebephrenic features

she says she wants to be
left alone and be allowed
to go back to school
that the hospital is making
her worse
and she has now lost all
her friends

sounds as though she is
beginning to rationalize
her own failures and to be
developing,
typically,
a paranoid
inflection to her thinking

In view of the above, 'treatment'—the inverse isometric diametric opposite of therapy—consists of
1.   hospitalization   against her wish she is put away
                          in order to be prevented
                          from slipping away

2.   early prevention, arrest of pathological process
      by
(i)   stopping her staring at the wall
      instead of letting her, even encouraging her
(ii) stopping her finding tranquillity,
      by giving her 'tranquillizers'.
(iii) damaging her brain, and disordering her mind,
      by giving her a course of electric shocks (eight)
(iv) chemically gripping her puberty,
      by hormones
to induce menstruation and pump up the development

of her breasts because she may be *organically* retarded in maturing (as 'schizophrenics' are often supposed to be).

She has not *complained* about these matters, but she cannot be expected to know what to complain about, otherwise why would she be in the hospital?

It is likely that she has an 'unconscious' sense of failure and inferiority because she has not been 'dated' and tumbled by any boys, because her breasts have not developed and she has not menstruated.

Besides she is not *interested* in boys. By chemically inducing sexual changes, she might be given a biological 'thrust' in an outward direction at a critical moment in her life cycle.

7 Oct. 1973, London

male TV commentator (middle-aged):

'. . . she won a few races last year
then she had twins
and of course
twins are no good for racing
so they were got rid of,

and now she's racing again
and I make her the favourite for this race
and the very best of luck to her,
now,
and in her future career . . .'

I thought at first he was talking about
a woman athlete
but he was talking about a racehorse
However,
a racehorse today
a woman
         tomorrow
                    what's the difference?

10 / The Scientific Method and Us

> Those that would gain what is under heaven by
> tampering with it—
> I have seen that they do not succeed. For that
> which is under heaven is like a holy vessel,
> dangerous to tamper with.
> Those that tamper with it, harm it.
> Those that grab it, lose it.
>
> —*Tao Te Ching* *

'I used to be an obstetrician,' Dr. William Masters
said, 'which is boring 90 per cent of the time. So every
time I delivered a boy I used to engage in a little con-
test to see if I could cut the cord before he had an
erection. I won about 50 per cent of the time.' †

The scientific method is based on tampering with
what would be happening if we were doing nothing to
it.
   Scientific interference is potentially the most destructive interference. Only a scientist knows *how* to interfere most destructively.

Love reveals *facts* which, without it, remain undis-
closed.

* Translated by Arthur Waley, George Allen and Unwin,
London, 1965.
   † *International Herald Tribune*, Paris, 7 May 1973, p. 6.

A heartless intellect can do no other than investigate the hell of its own hellish constructions by its own hellish instruments/instrumentality/methods, and to describe, in the language of hell
its own hellish conclusions/findings/hypotheses.

> The cure comes from the medicine,
> and the art of medicine
> originates in charity.
>
> Hence,
> to be cured is not a work of Faith,
> but one of sympathy.
>
> The true ground of medicine
> is love.
>
> —Paracelsus *

We should not needlessly multiply (hypothetical) entities seems to be an excellent principle.†

In modern scientific theory and practice, an attitude is often encountered which takes its justification from this principle, but which I do not believe has anything to do with it.

This is, to discount the *existence* of X because we have no hypothesis to account for it, or because science has not verified it, or because science cannot prove it, and sometimes, even, because science cannot *dis*prove it.

Or again, to see no value in X, because present scientific theory cannot find any value in it.

Some scientists are unable to conceive that by their

---

* Quoted by Henry M. Pachter, *Paracelsus: Magic into Science*, Collier Books, New York, 1961, pp. 121, 152.
† Occam's razor: 'Entia non sunt multiplicanda praeter necessitatem.'

methods they screen out the type of information they do not want, in order to bring into outline the type of information they do.

However if they look at the scientific information they get, forgetting to look at it in the light of the fact that the net of the scientific method does not actually catch the ocean upon which it is cast, they reduce themselves to intellectual idiocy.

Here is a well-known neuroscientist who has for years specialized in cutting brains in two, showing how his two hemispheres work after his years of research.*

'Space in the intracranial region is tight, and one wonders if the premium item could not have been utilized for better things than the kind of right-left duplication that now prevails. Evolution, of course, has made notable errors in the past, and one suspects that in the elaboration of the higher brain centers evolutionary progress is more encumbered than aided by the bilateralized scheme which, of course, is deeply entrenched in the mechanisms of development and also in the basic wiring plan of the lower nerve centres.' Sperry added that he felt the human head could probably do very well with a 'single unified set of brain controls'.

'With the existing cerebral system,' he said, 'most memories have to be laid down twice—one engram for the left hemisphere and another engram copy for the right hemisphere. The amount of information stored in memory in a mammalian brain is a remarkable thing in itself; to have to double it all for the second hemisphere would seem in many ways a bit wasteful. It is doubtful that all this redundancy has had any direct survival value . . .''

* R. W. Sperry, quoted by Leonard A. Stevens, *Explorers of the Brain*, Alfred A. Knopf, New York, 1971, p. 306.

I sometimes feel, in reviewing the evidence on the localization of the memory trace, that the necessary conclusion is that learning just is not possible. It is difficult to conceive of a mechanism which can satisfy the conditions set for it. Nevertheless, *in spite of such evidence against it* [italics mine], learning does sometimes occur.

—K. S. Lashley, 'In Search of the Engram' (1950)*

Nevertheless

We are beginning to have some reasonable guesses as to the 'gadgets' [still in quotation marks] that would serve as a memory mechanism—guesses sufficiently concrete to permit testing by rigorous experimentation. I think it is realistic to hope for *an understanding of memory precise enough to permit experimental modification of it in men.*

Ralph Gerard (1953)†

Half the patients in all hospitals in the United States are there for trouble in their brains. In Illinois a third of all State hospital inhabitants have senile psychoses. Pray for their speedy death or legislate for euthanasia, but waste no tears on them. They had their chance.

Everything we learn of organisms leads us to conclude not merely that they are analogous to machines but that they are machines. Man-made machines are not brains, but brains are a very ill-understood variety of computing machines. Cybernetics has helped to pull down the wall between the great world of physics and the ghetto of the mind.

So long as we, like good empiricists, remember that it is an act of faith to believe our senses, that

* Quoted by L. A. Stevens, op. cit., p. 293.
† *Readings from Scientific American Psychobiology*, W. H. Freeman, San Francisco, 1967.

we corrupt but do not generate information, and that our most reputable hypotheses are but guesses open to refutation, so long may we 'rest assured that God has not given us over to thraldom under that mystery of iniquity, of sinful man aspiring to the place of God.*

No, we may not rest assured.

* Warren S. McCulloch, *Embodiments of Mind*, MIT Press, Cambridge, Mass., 1965, pp. 276, 163, 164.

11 / A Lecture

Charles Sherrington, one of the great physiologists of the early twentieth century, proposed that man is a biochemical complex with certain ways of its own, but chemical nonetheless. His major work in physiology consisted of the exploration of the reflex arc and the attempt to establish the nature and function of the central nervous system. In his major technical monograph on the subject (*The Integrative Action of the Nervous System*), he proposed that our nervous system serves the function of integrating the different parts of itself and of the body. In his Gifford lectures, 'Man on His Nature', he took as an epigraph a quotation from Samuel Taylor Coleridge, in which Coleridge speaks of the nature of an organism as a system in which the whole is implied in each of the parts. Sherrington's method was vivisection, a method that goes back in the West at least to the Greeks. Galen came across a man who could move his body around without any apparent impediment, but who had lost his sensory feedback. He then showed experimentally that there were two sets of pathways in the body, and postulated that there must be a set of nerves going out (motor) and a set of nerves coming in (sensory). The idea was that nerves were very thin tubes, and something flowed along them in different directions. In order to confirm his clinical observations scientifically, Galen cut the spinal column of an animal into longitudinal sections (the front, the side, the back of it, and so on), and established that if these cuts were done in different places, there would be different responses from the

animal. That is, he cut a live animal into slices, and
did things to the slices to see what would happen.

In our physiology course, our first practical experiment was with frogs in a laboratory in which there
were about fifty to sixty students arranged along
benches. Half that number of live frogs had been set
out, and when our instructor gave us the word, we
had to take up these live frogs by their feet and smash
their heads simultaneously on the edge of the lab
benches. First we observed what that did to a frog.
It's been killed, but it still twitches. Then we systematically proceeded in a way that is described—I
can't help saying beautifully, though it still absolutely
freezes my heart when I read it—by William James in
the first chapter of his *Principles of Psychology*.

I want to explore the relation between my mind and
my brain. How shall I go about it? William James *
tells us that 'the best way to enter the subject' is 'to
take a lower creature, like a frog', and study, by cutting
it up *alive* into different bits, 'the functions of his different nerve-centres'. If you play around with the bits
attached to the spinal cord alone, their movements
'almost resemble in their machine-like regularity the
performance of a jumping-jack, whose legs must twitch
whenever you pull the string'.

If, then, we reduce the frog's nervous system to the
spinal cord alone, by making a section behind the base
of the skull, between the spinal cord and the medulla
oblongata, thereby cutting off the brain from all connection with the rest of the body, the frog will still
continue to live, but with a very peculiarly modified
activity. It ceases to breathe or swallow; it lies flat on

* *The Principles of Psychology*, Dover, New York, 1950,
vol. I, pp. 14–19.

its belly, and does not, like a normal frog, sit up on its fore paws, though its hind legs are kept, as usual, folded against its body and immediately resume this position if drawn out. If thrown on its back, it lies there quiety, without turning over like a normal frog. Locomotion and voice seem entirely abolished. If we suspend it by the nose, and irritate different portions of its skin by acid, it performs a set of remarkable 'defensive' movements calculated to wipe away the irritant. Thus, if the breast be touched, both fore paws will rub it vigorously; if we touch the outer side of the elbow, the hind foot of the same side will rise directly to the spot and wipe it. The back of the foot will rub the knee if that be attacked, whilst if the foot be cut away, the stump will make ineffectual movements, and then, in many frogs, a pause will come, as if for deliberation, succeeded by a rapid passage of the opposite unmutilated foot to the acidulated spot. . .

. . . The segment governing the arms is especially active, in male frogs, in the breeding season; and these members alone with the breast and back appertaining to them, everything else being cut away, will then actively grasp a finger placed between them and remain hanging to it for a considerable time.

And the same sort of thing in man. 'Robin, on tickling the breast of a criminal an hour after decapitation, saw the arm and hand move towards the spot.'

The upper centres give orders to the lower centres through a line of command.

'It is like a general ordering a colonel to make a certain movement, but not telling him how it shall be done.'

I hope if someone wanted to get to know me he would not smash my head, cut out my brain, take my head from my neck, cut my body in half, turn me upside down, burn me with acid, and torture the whole and all the bits with electricity and God knows what.

There is a vogue nowadays of chopping up worms into smaller and smaller bits, to see (among other things) how many different bits grow into new worms, who are then chopped into bits, in turn, and so *ad infinitum*.

I was fortunate as a student in Glasgow to have as teachers a number of people who had established themselves competently in this tradition. If we suppose that we are bits of chemical matter of some kind, we've got to take that flesh and blood and those nerves, and all the rest of it, and simply do everything we can imagine to it and see how it responds. The idea is to take these bits of chemical stuff and torment and torture them in any way you like so long as you try to predict beforehand what will happen, on the basis of what has happened before. You hope to be able to predict what will happen if I do this on the basis of a hypothesis you've formed from what happened when you did that. If you're good at that and lucky, you may get a Nobel Prize. Sir Charles Sherrington put his stamp on the reflex arc, though he did not invent it, and the reflex arc is a figure indelibly imprinted on the mind of every biology student. Unless you have familiarized yourself with that kind of thing in biology and in physiology, anatomy, pathology, in clinical neurology, in neuropsychiatry, you haven't a chance of becoming a doctor; you'd never pass the exams. Sir Charles Sherrington says somewhere in *The Integrative Action of the Nervous System* that actually the reflex arc is an experimental 'fiction', and he points out that there are many others. This one is one of the exports of the laboratory into all our lives: much of the theory and practice of education, of the 'programming' of behaviour therapy, is based on the notion that we *basically*, when it comes down to it, after one has had the nerve to discard the untestable opinions of unscientific philosophers and others untutored in science, are physical-chemical black boxes;

into this black box comes input, and out of it goes output. In between, some sort of central processing is going on, which is an elaboration of the in-between bits (which accounts for everything). Essentially, input comes in, is processed, and goes out.

The first piece of RAT research I came across was in the fifties. A biologist I knew was doing research with distant hopes of a Nobel Prize. Since he belonged to the left, he didn't think there was much chance of hitting a Nobel, though you never could tell. His work was to get rats under laboratory conditions and turn the heat down, colder and colder. The game was to see how cold you could get them before they would stop copulating. Now, he was a pure scientist, not an applied scientist. He had a permanent camera set up to film them 'at it.' Little bits of fluff would be given to them so that they could warm themselves up just a wee bit if they huddled together as tightly as possible. Even after they were deep-frozen stiff, when they got a little warmth back, they would still make love.

His was no trivial occupation. I often find it very difficult to realize that probably every major government in the world has stashed away, through vast underground labyrinths, food for those people the computer determines are to have priority for survival at the last roundup. But the rats are a menace because even in extreme cold, if there's still only a little bit of something they can huddle in, they can still keep it going. So it's a problem. Some of the best scientific minds are engaged in the rat race for the Nobel Prize on rat research.

I once spent a lifetime (when I woke up and found myself back in my bed, I couldn't decide for a while what was dream and what was 'reality') as a rat in the sewers of contemporary Tokyo. I ended my rat lifetime in a way that my rat consciousness couldn't make out, but it was something like bubonic plague. I began to swell up. Pus was oozing out of my blind eyes and all over the place. I staggered around, then collapsed, faded out, and faded back into my bed.

I must say, I preferred that death to the deaths meted out to some people I've seen in our hospitals.

I don't see how we can expect to get away with tormenting our fellow creatures in the ways we do without this heartless method effecting how we treat one another. Do animals have any moral status? When we 'apply' such theory to humans, we, at our gentlest, most humane, are led down the path of such procedures as 'behaviour modification'. The point of therapy is to get behaviour *out* of that sort of control (I should have thought), not to get it more efficiently technologically controlled.

When I was at medical school almost all my friends became psychiatrists, because it was the only bit of medicine we felt we could survive in, given what we saw as the prevalent the medico-surgical dehumanization of civilization.

One is not allowed into the 'inner' circles of Western medicine in hospitals as a mere pre-clinical medical student. Once you are allowed in, you've passed a major landmark, and now you work in the hospital. If you want to, as I did, you live in the hospital, perhaps for years. In my day the consulting surgeon came along, in pin-striped trousers and whatnot, on Monday morning and spoke to the registrar, also attired and moving in the appropriate manner, that professional bedside manner. He reminded me of Felix Krull, Thomas Mann's confidence trickster, who makes his way around different countries of Europe, with two or three words of French, two or three words of Italian, and gets by wherever he goes without having to say practically anything.

The Chief says, 'Well, what have we got in the ward today?' and the reply: 'Nothing but surgical trash, sir, I'm afraid. We've got a haemorrhoid in bed three, we've got a couple of veins, we've got a good gall bladder coming in tomorrow.'

'Ugh, ugh, what are we going to show the students?'

'Well, we've got a good anal prolapse. It doesn't have surgical interest, but it's a good teaching thing.'

Half a dozen or more students, for whom it's all new, follow him around the ward, all in white coats, all with stethoscopes and various other gadgets: 'Mr So-and-so, would you care to do a PR for us and tell us what you find on Mrs McLaughlin?' Mrs McLaughlin is a woman of fifty, who has come in because she's been losing a lot of weight and has abdominal pain. We were wondering if she might have a cancerous growth, and it will be interesting to see if one can feel it by putting a finger, with a rubber fitted around it, up her anus, and then moving it this way and that, noting when she squeals with pain. I shall resist the temptation to tell some of my medical horror stories. Every doctor has his batch. There was a lot of genuine humanity among the doctors and teachers and clinicians in Glasgow, but at its very best, medical training was bedevilled, and still is, by its own heartless theory. At least, so it seems to me. When I got to psychiatry I started to read the clinical descriptions. Textbooks describe inability to feel, lack of insight, imperviousness, robotization, mechanization, the loss of sense of feeling for quality, often self-confessed feelings of futility and meaninglessness. 'Schizoid' individuals maybe have 'insight', but it is without feeling, it's heartless; thinking may be precise, but it's without heart. When, as a medical student, I came across these descriptions in medical textbooks for the first time, I thought they were a very good description of medicine itself, including psychiatry. The heartlessness, the divorce, the split between head and heart. The fragmentation, indeed disintegration, behind all that, and its disavowal and projection. The unavailing cognitive efforts to put pieces together. The 'institutionally re-enforced' imperviousness of the cognitive scheme, the self-perpetuating, self-confirming nature of the process, which can never prove itself wrong by itself. Such descriptions seemed to me from the first moment I read them to be descriptions of the describers, as of the people they were trying to describe.

There was one full-length mirror in my home as a child, and I spent a lot of time looking into it. That's supposed in some quarters to be an early symptom of schizophrenia, or at least ominous. Along with many other things I did as a child. Mirrors are very important. Winnicott proposed that when a baby looks at its mother's face, the face is the baby's first mirror. It's in that face that one sees oneself reflected. The image one develops of one's own face is built up in very complex ways. Once it is established, I suppose many people feel they are somewhere or other behind a face which they can't see because they are on this side of it, but if they could see, if they could look into a mirror, or if they could get around in their imagination from behind and look at themselves from outside, then they would see their 'face'.

But what is one's original face before one is born? This face that we take to be our face is far from our original face, and if we identify ourselves with that face, then we're already in a sense deracinated, uprooted, and captured by this magic spell of reflected images reflecting each other, wherein we can become lost by identifying ourselves with any part of it. There's no way to describe one's original face. One can only allude. Some people go so far as to try to characterize their original face, but that is felt to be going too far by those who have gone further.

If I felt shaky, scattered, unaccountably frightened, or in any state of bewilderment or consternation or disarray or perplexity or confusion, and if I went to many a mental hospital looking for help, then I would be like the Aztecs rushing into the mouths of the Spanish cannon in hope of finding deliverance. If I really wanted to put myself in the position of being driven crazy, then the best way I can think of going about it is to go into one of those psychiatric institutions, mental hospitals, where psychiatric psychosis is in full swing, uncontested. In such places there is complete local power to chop and cut people up, physically as well as theoretically, in the name of the exact opposite of what is said is being done. The error in some domains of psychiatry is not a casual one. It's an error of one hundred and eighty degrees in the opposite direction without insight.

Many of psychiatry's severest critics have themselves been psychiatrists. If it deals largely in fictions, these fictions are powerful social facts. Concepts used as mandates to do things to people are facts, like so many of the other facts of our social life: you could call them factoids or pseudofacts, like these other systems that grab a sufficient number of people to become endemic and then are accepted by perhaps the majority, for a time.

I do not assume that anyone who is diagnosed as psychotic or anything else is, *per se, ipso facto*, more or less crazy than the person—or computer—doing the diagnosing.

I am very interested in words, and what we have words for and what we haven't got words for. For instance, the word 'paranoia'. It seems very strange to me that we have this word which means, in effect, that someone feels that he is being persecuted when the people who are persecuting him don't think that he is. But we haven't got a word for the condition in which you are persecuting someone without realizing it, which I would have thought is as serious a condition as the other, and certainly no less common.

Electroshock therapy was being tried out in Glasgow when I was a medical student. Its introduction was bitterly opposed by some of the senior psychiatrists, including my first psychiatric teacher, Dr Sclare. He illustrated his objections by citing the case of a woman of twenty-six who had begun a career as a concert violinist. At the end of her first, very successful tour she had crashed into a depression, and it was felt it would be a pity if she didn't get going again fairly soon. So she got a course of electric shocks, which brightened her up. But unfortunately (one of the common side effects of these things), she forgot her violin repertoire. At least she couldn't remember it sufficiently to be able to play in concerts any more—ever. In those days (1949), in Glasgow, most of the senior psychiatrists wouldn't have anything to do with electric shocks, but they are very appealing today because they do often brighten people up and get them going again, walking and talking. One enthusiast in London goes around publicly giving figures of 85 per cent remission of symptoms in electric shock treatment for involutional depression, and comparable figures for all sorts of other conditions, including children who don't want to have anything to do with other people, seventeen-year-old hysterics, and so on. He gets 'very good results' so far as I hear. He comes around in the morning, does the ward rounds. 'How are you today? Better or worse?' And if you don't say you're better, you get another course of electric shock treatment. Most people say they are better, and most of them do not report back to the out-patient department.

I remember one case conference in which I 'presented', as a psychiatrist, a young man who was a patient at the Glasgow University Department of Psychiatry. The young man was suffering from a sense of futility. This is considered a symptom of schizoid personality disorder, along with derealization and depersonalization and so forth. He could find no meaning to life. After I'd given his 'history' and a short account of the patient, he was brought in and asked a few questions, and then sent out again. Around the table we (about a dozen psychiatrists, clinical psychologists, and social workers) discussed this 'case'. One question was the diagnosis, whether this patient was a schizoid personality, or whether he was possibly at the beginning of a schizophrenic process of deterioration. I ventured (this was in 1956) to remark that the question whether life was worth living had been taken up quite a bit in recent European literature, indeed one could find considerations of it all over the place. I did not think it was a foregone conclusion that the sense of futility betokened psychopathology.

After the conference the head of the department asked me to come to his office. He said that he thought there was something in what I said. Even he, a professor of psychiatry, could remember two occasions in his life when he had had 'attacks' of futility. One was when he was a colonel in the British army during the war, and was travelling a lot by train. As he looked out the window, very tired, he was overcome by a transient attack of futility. He put it down to the parallax phenomenon working on a fatigued CNS. His second attack had been when he was tying his left shoelace that very morning: as he bent down, he was overcome with a sense of futility. He is a very well-intentioned person, and I respect him and am fond of him, but he would rate in my book as in some respects more out of touch with reality than the patient was. Psychiatrists are people as well as patients. And so it is with so many people who are subjected to such an inundation of desperate people seeking their help, and feel helpless in the face of all this misery they are supposed to do something about. Such people are always dreaming of a 'break-through' in treatment.

When I was at the Glasgow Royal Mental Hospital, Gartnavel, I spent the best part of three months living, as much as I could, in the female refractory ward of the hospital. In that hospital, we had ladies' west and women's east and gentlemen's west and men's east, for the paying and non-paying patients respectively. In the female east admissions ward, a locked ward with the usual paraldehyde and bromide sedatives, I persuaded the hospital authorities to try an experiment of taking everyone off every drug that they didn't want. Thirty windows in that ward were broken during the first week. All were replaced, as they were broken, by the hospital maintenance staff, who were very glad to have something to do. The cost of replacing the broken glass was, I think, less than one tenth the cost of the drugs that these people were usually put 'under'.

When tranquillizers came in, however, they didn't smell like paraldehyde and didn't have the side effects of bromide, and they seemed both to quiet people and to make them more 'cooperative'. At a staff meeting with doctors and nurses, one of the nursing sisters asked about a somewhat wild woman. 'Do these new drugs have any effect on height?' she wondered. We asked what she meant, and she reported that she thought this woman had shrunk three inches since she had been on tranquillizers. I said that to the best of my knowledge, they didn't have any effect on height, but it was an observation I've continued to remember. I've often been asked by residents in hospitals to give a patient an injection when there might be some sort of life starting up in him, perhaps a crying or whimpering or yelling or screaming or not going to bed at the proper time, not getting up at the proper time, not coming to eat at the proper time, and so on. Doctors often feel that there is nothing they can do except to give the patient an injection to keep at least the staff calmer. They're not always terribly happy about it.

There's nothing that affects our chemistry more immediately than other people. When one walks into a room where one feels welcome and comfortable and so on, if one had a little trepidation before going in, that settles down, one's heart is not in a flurry, one's breathing is calm, one's palms are not sweating, one's throat isn't dry, one doesn't have butterflies in one's stomach. All these experiential affairs are inextricably part of the same tapestry as that of our chemistry. There's nothing more intimately attuned to how we feel in other people's company than our body chemistry. And I'm sure that just as there is a chemistry of acute fear, so there is a chemistry of chronic despair.

In the case of the wild woman, a chemical agent had modified her behaviour, and there was a reportable, measurable change in another person's perception, so that the person experienced her as smaller. Transformations induced by introducing a chemical agent inside the skin of one person included perceptual changes in other people who shared the same social system.

'Tranquillizers' are another import into our lives from the laboratory. They were drugs found to help people who were interested in controlling rats, rendering them more amenable and more cooperative. Chemical agents that enable rats to be controlled more efficiently are given to people for the same reason. Given a suitable selling name first, of course. You can't 'tranquillize' someone. Tranquillity cannot be imposed by a chemical. In recent years in the USA I've often been asked to 'do' an interview with a patient in front of other people. I have sometimes agreed, with the stipulation that the patient not be on tranquillizers. Out of the first eight occasions set up that way, not one psychiatric department could bring itself to present a patient to me who was regarded as psychotic but not on tranquillizers. The staff seem ashamed and terrified of anyone out of their control. In some quarters, as soon as anyone starts to *feel* anything, then they've got to be very careful just whom they tell, and how they go about manifesting it, and so on. According to my friend Ross Speck, who was professor of psychiatry at the Hahnemann Medical College in Philadelphia, the most common last straw leading to admission to mental hospitals in the United States in 1972 was—what would you think?—smashing the television set!

Gartnavel wasn't too bad as a genuine refuge. Many patients would admit themselves back there of their own accord. The dictum, when it was set up in the nineteenth century, was *no injurious treatment:* no injury was to be done to the patient in the name of his or her treatment—a very important principle. It *was* an asylum for some people; it depended on who was 'running' what wards, of course.

When I spent those months in the female refractory ward of the hospital, I did my other duties, but I spent most of my time, day and night, in that ward. There were about sixty patients, with two nurses at a time. A doctor examined each patient at statutory six-month intervals, when the patient was tucked tightly into bed, with screens around. The doctor would apply the stethoscope to see that she wasn't dying of pneumonia, and get out again as quickly as possible. It was impossible to ascertain how many people in that ward had had lobotomies in the last few years; they weren't even down in the case records. After three or four weeks, I was part of the life of that ward. No doctor ever entered the locked door without the telephone ringing from another ward to say that he was on his way. Then the nurse would come in and say, 'The doctor is coming', and everyone would take up their appropriate positions and start up their usual numbers. What the doctor then saw (including, presumably, the doctor who had been the superintendent of that hospital and who wrote one of the most commonly taught textbooks of psychiatry) bore little resemblance to what otherwise went on in that place.

After taking stock of this situation for three months, and being in full sympathy with the patients and with those nurses who took heart as soon as they saw just a possibility that this ghastly, dismal scene might possibly change, I wrote a report in which I put forward to the hospital management committee various recommendations for changing the different aspects of the institutional structure of the part of the hospital where I worked. In the first place, I pointed out that, in my view, it was quite clear from my observations that more important than my medication was the relationship between staff and patients, and the relationship between patients and other patients.

The nurses hadn't realized this themselves; they were taught that they had jobs to do, but that their 'jobs' didn't include being friendly with patients. They came on in shifts, were attached to a ward, and then might be shifted at a moment's notice to another ward. Say a nurse was getting along well with a few patients after being on one ward for a little while. She could disappear, never to appear again. She could be shifted without warning to another ward on the other side of the hospital, and that would be that. 'Her' patients were suddenly bereft of possibly their one lifeline to the outer world. Almost all the women had been locked up there for years. What they felt was considered meaningless, of course, because they're all crazy, that's why they're there. If their feelings were taken seriously, they couldn't be treated in the way they were (are).

I wrote a detailed, point-by-point report on the state of affairs at the hospital. I'd just come out of the British army where I was a captain and I wasn't frightened about being only twenty-six years old. I made a number of specific proposals of which several were adopted, and there was one that involved myself specifically. Sitting in the refractory ward, I concentrated on those people who were regarded as the most hopeless, who had been given up completely. I ascertained from the nurses whom they felt most hopeless about, and noted also whom the nurses and other patients left most alone, and who made fewest moves themselves toward others. All of the people on the ward had been hospitalized continually for at least six years, all of them were over thirty-five, and all were women. I drew up sociograms of the interplay of relationships on the ward, and I answered my own questions as to the most hopeless patients, the most withdrawn, the patients who were the most neglected, those whom other patients had least to do with, and those who reacted least and did least.

The twelve most hopeless patients were selected by these criteria. There were a couple of other people on the hospital staff at the time who also were hopeful about change, including the assistant matron. It was agreed that these twelve patients would have two nurses whose sole duty, I insisted, would be to have them as their flock. It wasn't possible to obtain all of the conditions I'd hoped for, but what was possible was to have these two nurses assigned on a promise for at least a year, if they wanted to stick it out, to be with these patients from nine in the morning till five at night. The

hours were at the matron's insistence. And not on week-
ends. I said to the nurses that I wasn't going to worry
about whether they went on duty at nine or left at
five—you can't do these things that way—but that they
should just be with these people as much as they could
take. If they couldn't take it, this should not cost them
promotion, loss of face, or so on. The other stipulation
was that the patients have their own room. I couldn't
get a twenty-four-hour-a-day room, but I did get a
rather pleasant room, simply laid out. It wasn't a ward;
there were no beds in it. And so the twelve patients
and two nurses went to that room from nine in the
morning till five in the evening.

On the first day, the twelve 'completely withdrawn'
patients had to be shepherded from the ward across to
the day room. The second day, at half past eight in the
morning, I had one of the most moving experiences of
my life on that ward. There they all were clustered
around the locked door, just waiting to get out and
get over there with the two nurses and me. And they
hopped and skipped and twiddled around and whatnot
on their way over. So much for being 'completely withdrawn'.

I left that hospital about a year later. The project
was continued, in modified form, after I left. In eighteen
months from the start, all twelve patients had left the
hospital. In another year all twelve were back again.
The experiment petered out, but at the time it made a
difference to the twelve people and two nurses, and to
a lot of others. Many other aspects of the hospital took
on a somewhat different complexion to the staff.
Nothing succeeds like success. It worked while it lasted,
and did not cost anything.

Today, they're cutting up children and putting de-
vices into unborn babies. The statistics for the number
of women to men whose brains have been cut up in
America are 3 to 1, all *by* men. About twenty generations back in Europe, 100,000 women a year, a very
large percentage of the population in those days, were
being picked up in their beds in the middle of the

night, without warning, stripped of all their clothes, thrown into a cart, and then trundled off into the inquisitorial European dungeons. There, after starvation and kicking about a bit, they'd be subject to torture, interrogation, and burning. Twenty generations back, that's what was going on. These women came from all classes, from the top to the bottom of the social structure, your grannies and mine, grannies grannies grannies, sometimes young girls, sometimes aged, married or single, tortured and burnt. This is just to put a little bit of social and historical perspective on what's happening now. It's done so neatly today that most people don't know it's happening.

Respect, courtesy, gentleness, kindness, consideration, compassion, charity: I believe we all know what these terms mean. They do not preclude technique and technology. Over twenty years ago, in my humble capacity as a young doctor, one of my jobs was to keep brain-dead human heart-lung 'preparations' alive longer than anyone else. A surgical team (was it in Stockholm or Tokyo?) had kept someone with almost total erasure of the brain, even with a lot of midbrain damage, alive for a couple of years. I don't know whether one would say 'alive' or not. If you are sufficiently smart at this, with appropriate 'drips' and so forth, you can keep the heart pumping and the lungs going on almost indefinitely it seems, just for, as we would say, the sake of science. The game was playing with human flesh to see who would have the best report to make at the next International Congress of Neurosurgery.

Such technology is demonic, but technology needn't be like that. We can have all the technology we want, and it can be even more precise, more accurate, and much better than now, and we can put it all into the woodwork when we want to, as a back-up for life, not to mangle life by it, or to turn ourselves into very inefficient computers. I wouldn't even try to compete with computers or with anything that a computer does, any more than I would try to compete with a crane. I can't do that. But to be sent to school and university and medical school in order to turn oneself into a very inefficient type of computer is total nonsense. We can have the technology, but if it's heartless, forget it. Speaking about being openhearted is not a matter of being 'romantic' or 'back-to-nature' or 'humanities' or any other of the stereotypes people sometimes respond with if one talks about the heart. It's a matter of common sense, God help us all.

Old and New Information about Electroshock

*Ugo Cerletti M.D.**

Convulsions were to be induced with a therapeutic aim since the good clinical results obtained by Meduna's method were ascribed to them. For this the old transcranial method followed by physiologists was sufficient. But this idea then, and for a long time to come, appeared Utopian, because of the terror with which the notion of subjecting a man to high-tension currents was regarded. The spectre of the electric chair was in the minds of all and an imposing mass of medical literature enumerated the casualties, often fatal, ensuing upon electric discharges across the human body. Nowadays, after twelve years of experience with electroshock, that terror may seem to have been exaggerated; but cases of death caused by low tensions (forty volts) had been described. Since, to obtain fits in dogs, tensions of around 125 volts were used, moreover with an alternating current—which was held to be more dangerous than direct—it seemed evident that these experiments were too near the danger zone to have any possibility of being applied to man. The fact is that no one at the clinic seriously thought of applying electric convulsions *to man,* even though experiments continued upon dogs,

* *American Journal of Psychiatry,* 107/2, August 1950, pp. 87–94.

both with electricity and with Cardiazol. So, over a year went by.

Nevertheless I, who had gone to such lengths in striving to preserve dogs from death when given electrically induced convulsions, had now come to the conviction that a discharge of electricity must prove equally harmless to a man if the duration of the current's passage were reduced to a minimum interval. Continually turning the problem over in my mind I felt that I would sooner or later be able to solve it; so much so that in 1937, not being able to go to the Munsingen Congress, I allowed Bini to hint at these vague hopes, and I myself, at the 1937 Milan Assembly concerning the therapeutics of schizophrenia, announced these hopes that I had been nourishing.

This inactivity in the face of so momentous a question greatly depressed me, so that I immediately jumped at the information, given me by my colleague, Professor Vanni, that 'at the Rome slaughterhouse pigs are killed by electricity'. As though to justify my passiveness and to settle my hopes by facing a real fact, I decided to see this electric slaughtering with my own eyes, and immediately went to the slaughterhouse.

There I was told that the application of a current across the pigs' heads had been in use for some years. The butchers took hold of the pigs near their ears with a large scissor-shaped pair of pincers. The pincers were connected to the lighting plant with wires, and terminated in two teethed disc-electrodes enclosing a sponge wet with water. As they were seized, the pigs fell on their sides and were soon taken by fits (convulsed). Then the butcher, taking advantage of the unconscious state of the animal, gave its neck a deep slash, thus bleeding it to death.

I at once saw that the fits were the same as those I had been producing in dogs, and that these pigs were not being 'killed by electricity', but were bled to death during the epileptic coma.

Since a great number of pigs was available at the slaughterhouse for killing, I now set myself the exact opposite of my former experiments' aims; namely, no longer to make efforts to keep the convulsed animals alive, but rather to determine what the conditions must be for obtaining their death by an electric current. Having obtained authorization for experimenting from the director of the slaughterhouse, Professor Torti, I carried out tests, not only subjecting the pigs to the current for ever-increasing periods of time, but also applying the current in various ways: across the head, across the neck, and across the chest. Various durations (twenty, thirty, sixty or more seconds) were tried. It turned out that the more serious results (prolonged apnea sometimes lasting many minutes and, exceptionally, death) appeared when the current crossed the chest; that this application was not mortal for durations of some tenths of a second; and, finally, that passage of the current across the head, even for long durations, did not have serious consequences. It was found that pigs, even when treated in this last way several times, 'came to' gradually, after a fairly long interval (five to six minutes), then started moving, next made various attempts to get shakily to their feet, and finally ran rapidly to mix with their mates in the pen.

These clear proofs, certain and oft repeated, caused all my doubts to vanish, and without more ado I gave instructions in the clinic to undertake, next day, the experiment upon man. Very likely, except for this fortuitous and fortunate circumstance of pigs' pseudo-electrical butchery, electroshock would not yet have been born.

A schizophrenic of about forty, whose condition was organically sound, was chosen for the first test. He expressed himself exclusively in an incomprehensible gibberish made up of odd neologisms, and since his arrival from Milan by train without a ticket, not a thing had been ascertainable about his identity.

Preparations for the experiment were carried out in an atmosphere of fearful silence bordering on disapproval in the presence of various assistants belonging to the clinic and some outside doctors.

As was our custom with dogs, Bini and I fixed the two electrodes, well wetted in salt solution, by an elastic band to the patient's temples. As a precaution, for our first test, we used a reduced tension (seventy volts) with a duration of 0.2 second. Upon closing the circuit, there was a sudden jump of the patient on his bed with a very short tensing of all his muscles; then he immediately collapsed onto the bed without loss of consciousness. The patient presently started to sing at the top of his voice, then fell silent. It was evident from our long experience with dogs that the voltage had been held too low.

I, bearing in mind the observations with repeated applications of the day before upon pigs, made arrangements for a repetition of the test.

Someone got nervous and suggested whisperingly that the subject be allowed to rest; others advised a new application to be put off to the morrow. Our patient sat quietly in bed, looking about him. Then, of a sudden, hearing the low-toned conversation around him, he exclaimed—no longer in his incomprehensible jargon, but in so many clear words and in a solemn tone —'Not *a second*. Deadly!'

The situation was such, weighted as it was with responsibility, that this warning, explicit and unequivocal, shook the persons present to the extent that some began to insist upon suspension of the proceedings. Anxiety lest something that amounted to superstition should interfere with my decision urged me on to action. I had the electrodes reapplied, and a 110-volt discharge was sent through for 0.5 second. The immediate, very brief cramping of all the muscles was again seen; after a slight pause, the most typical epileptic fit began to take place. True it is that all had their hearts in their mouths and were truly oppressed during the tonic phase with apnea, ashy paleness, and cadaverous facial cyanosis—an apnea which, if it be awe-inspiring in a spontaneous epileptic fit, now seemed painfully never-ending—until at the first deep, stertorous inhalation, and first clonic shudders, the blood ran more freely in the bystanders' veins as well; and lastly, to the immense relief of all concerned, was witnessed a characteristic, gradual awakening 'by steps'. The patient sat up of his own accord, looked about him calmly with a vague smile, as though asking what was expected of him. I asked him: 'What has been happening to you?' He answered, with no more gibberish: 'I don't know; perhaps I have been asleep.'

That is how the first epileptic fit experimentally induced in man through the electric stimulus took place. So electroshock was born; for such was the name I forthwith gave it. . . .

Bini in 1942 suggested the repetition of ECT many times a day for certain patients, naming the method 'annihilation'. This results in severe amnesic reactions that appear to have a good influence in obsessive states, psychogenic depressions and even in some paranoid cases. 'Clustering' of treatments, shocking daily for three or four days followed by a three-day rest, is less intense but sometimes effectual. The method of annihilation has made possible studies of amnesia and of hallucinations, delirium, and moria occurring during the treatment, relating them to the personality factors in the patients (Bini and Bazzi, Polimanti). Flescher and Virgili have made systematic researches on amnesia and showed that spontaneous memory is more damaged than that of learned, didactic material and that automatic memory is still less disturbed. Depressed and aged patients show disturbances earlier than young or excited patients. The 'annihilation syndrome' has been compared by Cerquetelli and Catalano with the psychopathology following prefrontal leukotomy. They indicate close parallelism with the advantage of reversibility in the case of shock.

These authors have also used shock successively to stop the symptoms of demerol mania quickly, following Martinotti who used it with success in other forms of toxicomania. Broggi and others have also used ECT in progressive paralysis with at least temporary success. Ruggeri has used ECT in Parkinsonism and DeCrinis in disseminated sclerosis, observing attenuation of hypertonia.

Electroshock has also been applied in certain general physical illnesses though all have a constitutional 'nervous' background. Recovery has been frequently reported in asthma, and Catalano and Cerquetelli, with Tommasi, have had success in psoriasis, prurigo, and alopecia areata. Mancioli, after having observed improvement in ozena in a schizophrenic patient treated with shock, found similar improvement after acroagonine injection and is pursuing the research with histological controls.

Two other ideas both of which have perhaps as much relation to poetry as to science must be mentioned. The first is simply that the word 'shock' does not have the same meaning in neuropsychiatry as in general pathology. It is worth noting that many of our therapeutic methods such as prolonged sleep, narcoanalysis, insulin coma, epileptic coma, electronarcosis, etc., have in common the factor of the induction of a state of unconsciousness.

The second idea has to do with the patient's fear of therapy, which leads some to want to stop it. On being asked the reason, they reply: 'I don't know, I am afraid.' 'Afraid of what?' 'I don't know, I have fear.' 'But were you worried, did you feel pain?' 'No, but I have fear.' There must be a vague recollection—organic memory—of the first 'terror-defence' reaction. I believe that name 'terror-defence' expresses the biological significance of epileptic fits. The terror phase, although taking place during unconsciousness, leaves specific bio-chemical and psychological changes in the organism that later emerge generically into the conscious sphere. This, too, was expressed long ago by Padre Dante,

'Qual e colui che somniando vede,
E dope il sogno la passione impressa
Rimane, e l'altro alla mente non riede. . .
(Para. XXXIII, 58–61)

(As he who while dreaming sees,
And after the dream is over,
The emotion remains while the picture has
    faded away. . .)

12 / Field Notes

Nov. 1972, Cafeteria, Buffalo Airport. c. 9.00 am

BLACK WAITRESS	(to white man who is bugging her) put me into the black void where you will not bother me
ME	put you where?
SHE	the black void. V-O-I-D. void. from where you are reborn
ME	black?
SHE	that's how I picture it
ME	do you remember it?
SHE	just as I picture it, sir.

Nov. 1972

	Notice in New York taxicab No smoking Driver allergic
ME	(to lady taxidriver) ten years ago there would have been something the matter with you, if you couldn't stand your lungs being poisoned
SHE	yeah. Not now. It's a filthy habit
ME	why do you think people smoke?
SHE	it's a detensifier
ME	oh. How do you mean?
SHE	they have to have something in their mouths

ME	why?
SHE	I think it's a habit from the breast, maybe they didn't get enough of it then. Of course I'm not a so-called expert. But that's what I think. What do you think?
ME	yes I think it's something like that. Seems very likely to me.

Nov. 1972, The Manger, Tampa, Florida 7.30 pm

An extensive lawn in the hotel grounds, of dark green *plastic* (!) grass.

Nov. 1972, Hotel Utah, Salt Lake City

Danny and I began to get desperate for some real food. All the milk is homogenized. All the fruit is chemicalized. Nothing but dyed buttermilk. The cheeses are all chemicalized one way or another. Just a mouthful of real bread, at least! We scoured the town in a taxi. Taken to (according to the taxi driver) the only health food shop in town. Only frozen, presliced 'health-food' bread, in cellophane

14 Nov. 1972, in flight Buffalo to Chicago

STEWARDESS	are you R. D. Laing?
ME	yes
STEWARDESS	I majored in psychology at Duke
ME	really
STEWARDESS	are you interested in ESP?
ME	well, er, I sort of grew up with it in Scotland
STEWARDESS	do you think it's been *cultured out*?
ME	I haven't heard that expression before

STEWARDESS	cultured out?
ME	maybe, maybe not forever

Dec. 1972, New Orleans

Saved. Food at last. Real coffee at last.

Dec. 1972, in flight New Orleans to Washington

I had taken my shoes and socks off.

STEWARDESS	(indicating my feet) is anything the matter sir?
ME	no
STEWARDESS	I'm sorry there is a regulation that all passengers must have adequate covering over their feet
ME	oh I'm sorry. Excuse me. I didn't know (putting on shoes and socks)
STEWARDESS	thank you sir
ME	I didn't know there was such a regulation

We developed a friendly chat. She told me that since a little girl she had never ever allowed her bare feet to touch the ground or the earth, neither bathing, nor coming out of a bath, nor going in and out of bed.

Oct. 1973, Venice c. 10.00 am

A clutch of affluent women, with clichéd faces
one of them spots a shop window,
with barely a glance at the window,
she calls out:

1ST WOMAN	Mabel, come here, it's fantastic!!

MABEL   (goes over, and turns her glutted eyes
               to the window: a clear moment *before*
               her eyes have contacted the window
               display, she shouts out)
               fantastic!!!

I used this vignette in several lectures to illustrate
the thesis that we live within, or can easily come to
live within, a skein of words,
    such that we see, as it were, other people's descrip-
tions of the world,
    instead of describing what we see. Other people
(like the first woman) are not 'seeing' the world either,
very often.
    the map is not the territory,
    the menu is not the meal, etc.
but that mote in one's own eye(s)!

JUTTA   (driving through fantastic scenery)
               isn't it fantastic scenery
ME   (with cursory turn of head) *fantastic!*

NATASHA   (new dress) do you like it?
ME   (writing) yes, it's very nice
NATASHA   how do you know? You haven't seen it
               yet (I had forgotten to look up)

Jan. 1973, Auckland to Honolulu 11.30 am

He used to be an obstetrician, he tells me. Now he
is the Chief of the Research and Development Department of one of the transworld chemical industries. His
department has a thirty-six million dollar a year budget.
    employs ninety-eight PhDs, and over thirty
    MDs, and in addition, gives
    grants for research to many university depart-
    ments throughout the world.

We were introduced in the First Class Airport Lounge by the host, and are now sitting together, knocking back Scotch on the rocks.

He is very interested in the chemical key to schizophrenia. Feels a breakthrough may not be far off. Has noted my name in the bibliographies. One of his daughters said to him he ought to read some of my stuff.

HE	I have two daughters. I've trained them both not to be interested in sex. Both are 'top' in their different academic fields now.
ME	are they?
HE	what?
ME	interested in sex?
HE	no. Both are safely married. I used to be a surgeon. I gave it up. But I do what I can from where I'm at.
ME	you must have gone through the Second World War then.
HE	it was disheartening, yes. That had something to do with it. Were you in it?
ME	I just missed it. I learned my neurology from a chap who had been Chief of the British Army's No. 1 Field Brain Surgery Unit through Africa and Italy. Eighteen hours a day sometimes.
HE	I was in Burma. We had a Jap brought in. We offered a thousand dollars for a live Jap. They were wanted for interrogation.
ME	offered to whom?
HE	the boys. Almost impossible to get one in alive. This one already had four punctures from bayonets in his stomach. But he was alive. So they got their thousand dollars. They 'interrogated' him and got what they wanted. I spent three and a half hours resecting yards of bowel, etc. He was carried out on a

	stretcher. Two shots. The sergeant came in and saluted: 'Prisoner shot trying to escape sir.'
ME	that's it
HE	that's it
	(another couple of Scotches on the rocks)
HE	our speciality was assembling and wrapping up our Surgical Theatre tent in twenty minutes
	two hundred million people suffer from schistosomiasis—ten years' expectancy
ME	I didn't know that
HE	one hundred per cent of the population behind two of the big dams suffer from it
ME	really?
HE	yes we have developed a drug. It's less toxic than the parasite. We laid out the red carpet for two ministers of health. Told them about it. They didn't want to know. Said it would land them with overpopulation.
ME	so?
HE	R & D is all right. But we have to have a market.
ME	sure
HE	no one would bite. Hell. I thought that was a shame. I thought if we could just do one production run—the stuff would at least be there.
ME	no buyers
HE	we did do one run. The American Army funded it. In case they might wish to move their troops sometime into a schistosomiasis area. The stuff's there. That's all I could do.
	(another two Scotches)
	you're a psychiatrist?
ME	yes

HE   you know that one about the guy who goes into the same bar every evening for twenty years and has two drinks?

ME   no

HE   he goes into the same bar every evening for twenty years and has two drinks. One night he goes into the bar as usual, has two drinks, and pees on the bar. OK the barman overlooks it. This guy's been coming here for twenty years. Next night. The same. Two drinks and pees on the bar. The barman says: 'Go see my cousin Herman. He's a psychiatrist. He'll sort you out.' He disappears for six months. Then comes back and says to the barman: 'I've been to see your cousin Herman. He sorted me out.' Has two drinks and pees on the bar. 'I thought you said my cousin Herman sorted you out?' 'Yes. I know why.'

ME   what's the why of all this Watergate business?

HE   Watergate is an extreme left-wing conspiracy. They are after him because they have never forgiven him for getting Alger Hiss. Douglas is a metastasis. But Nixon's next Supreme Court appointment should secure things for the next eighteen years.

ME   how about the trade unions? how infiltrated (by metastases from extreme left-wing cancer)?

HE   they are still quite wholesome. We arranged a strike recently.

ME   between?

HE   Union leadership and Management. Gives a good impression to the membership that the leadership is strong. They like to feel it's strong. I don't see any extreme left-wing takeover in the unions.

ME   maybe Kissinger is a communist agent

HE   you never can tell these days. The CIA is infiltrated with communists. You have to have a very suspicious mind to follow the moves these days.

I've read Marx. There's a lot in what he says. He would be right if people were idealists. But that's not the nature of the beast.

(two more of the same)

the newspapers, TV: they are all infiltrated. Do you know that *Time* and *Newsweek* have been bought up by the extreme left wing?

ME   have you been to China?

HE   no. I'm still suspicious of China. But we exchange scientific information. They are right there in analytical chemistry. Twenty years ahead of the Russians. We're just marketing a pill that's about six years behind the one they have had out for some time. How do they do it when they are so cut off!!

ME   maybe they think we're cut off

HE   the trouble with Americans is that they are so self-destructive. We licked the Japs and the Germans. Then let ourselves be taken advantage of. The trouble was Potsdam. Roosevelt was senile and surrounded by extreme left-wing infiltrators.

(pause for mutual reflection)

have you read Tolkien?

ME   no

HE   he's behind a lot of the way young people's minds are working. I can't make head or tail of him.

Feb. 1973, Harrison Hot Springs

MASSEUR	Yes, Mr. Laing, right we are (starts massage, stops, goes to appointment book, spells out L-A-I-N-G, comes back) you're not R. *D.* Lang
LAING	R. D. *Laing*
MASSEUR	you're not R. D. *Lang*
LAING	R. D. *LAING*
MASSEUR	you're not R. D. *LANG* the writer? (the massage becomes unpleasant and gets more so to the end)
LAING	as a matter of fact, I suppose I have to say I am
MASSEUR	no you're not. This is no laughing matter. (pause) no you are not
LAING	(I have been face down—I turn around on one elbow and say to him menacingly) I am not asking you to believe me (pause; silence; I lie down again— massage continues in cold silence)
MASSEUR	(quivering through his effort to 'watch it') what are you doing this weekend?
LAING	(I had to make a decision. I decided I would go on with this up to a point, but felt too vulnerable face down, so I turned over.) that'll do for that; just a little this way
MASSEUR	what are you doing this weekend?
LAING	I'm doing a workshop
MASSEUR	where?
LAING	in Vancouver
MASSEUR	it's not in Vancouver
LAING	I don't know where it is, somewhere around there
MASSEUR	I wanted to go but they said I wasn't qualified

LAING   I'm sorry

MASSEUR   and I couldn't afford the fees
(it's getting worse:
he hates me if I'm *not* R. D. Laing,
        for leading him on
and he hates me if I am . . .)

LAING   (mutters) I've been here before

MASSEUR   pardon

LAING   nothing
(pause)

MASSEUR   how do I know you're R. D. LANG?

LAING   that's not my problem

MASSEUR   (pleading—menacingly) R. D. Lang
wrote books

LAING   have you read any?

MASSEUR   no

LAING   I wrote *The Divided Self, Self and
Others, Sanity, Madness and the Family,
The Politics of Experience, Knots, The
Politics of* . . . (He does not recognize
any of them)

MASSEUR   R. D. LANG wrote *The Bird of Paradise*

LAING   I wrote *The Bird of Paradise*
(silence)
(He may kill me)

MASSEUR   are you a doctor?

LAING   yes

MASSEUR   a *real* doctor?

LAING   yes
(silence—massage ends
I am putting on robe to go)

MASSEUR   (suddenly) I have to kill time here so
I wanted to learn English literature; I
was going to start with Gertrude Stein
and you, and someone else I can't remember

LAING   Shakespeare?

MASSEUR   I can't remember. What do you think?

LAING	The Bible and Shakespeare—that's what I was brought up on
MASSEUR	so what do you think?
LAING	what do you want to study English literature for?
MASSEUR	to improve my mind
LAING	well er I'm sorry I have to go now, Cheerio
MASSEUR	what do you think?

Oct. 1974, On the train from London to Scotland

	Getting pissed at the bar with sundry 'other' ranks from a Scottish regiment. (round of drinks)
ME	Ireland must be tough
1ST SOLDIER	the worst thing about Ireland, you know what it is?
ME	tell me
1ST SOLDIER	while you're there you're restricted to two pints of beer a day and when you come back
2ND SOLDIER	you lash out
3RD SOLDIER	you blow it
1ST SOLDIER	it's normal isn't it
2ND SOLDIER	it's natural
3RD SOLDIER	it's fuckin inevitable (round of drinks)
1ST SOLDIER	my ambition in life, you know what it is?
ME	tell me
1ST SOLDIER	find a white woman and a black man in bed and put a grenade between them (general round of applause and approval) (round of drinks)
2ND SOLDIER	look at him
3RD SOLDIER	he's fuckin looking fuckin miserable
4TH SOLDIER	Aye why not?

2ND SOLDIER	didn't you shoot your load in London?
4TH SOLDIER	oh aye, this morning
2ND SOLDIER	and you've got a missus waiting for you?
ME	does she know you're on your way?
4TH SOLDIER	I haven't told her I'm coming (general sympathetic laughter and shaking of heads) (round of drinks)
4TH SOLDIER	if I catch her with a man
ME	kill him or beat her up?
4TH SOLDIER	beat her up definitely. definitely. Fuck it definitely.
A SAILOR	why should it be any different for her?
1ST SOLDIER	it's fuckin different mate
2ND SOLDIER	you just shoot your load and you're off (general assent)
1ST SOLDIER	she opens her legs
4TH SOLDIER	that's it
2ND SOLDIER	she receives it. You just shoot your load.
SAILOR	still we do it, why shouldn't they?
1ST SOLDIER	there's no right and wrong
4TH SOLDIER	I'm no angel
ME	no one suggested you were
2ND SOLDIER	it's different for a woman
SAILOR (TO 4TH SOLDIER)	you should have married a man
1ST SOLDIER	Aw fuck
2ND SOLDIER	maybe
4TH SOLDIER	it's not so simple (another round)
SAILOR	they're another species they're another fuckin species

What Is?

Plato's dialogue *The Parmenides** ends this way

PARMENIDES Let thus much be said; and further let us
affirm what seems to be the truth, that,
whether one is or is not, one and the
others in relation to themselves and one
another, all of them, in every way, are
and are not, and appear to be and appear
not to be.

ARISTOTELES Most true.

One is coerced in the movement of the dialogue to
agree with Aristoteles to this, I find most disquieting,
conclusion, since one is forced either to jump off by
denying the validity of one's own thought or, continuing
to think, to be forced to a conclusion my thought, at
least, does not like.

David Hume and a few others seem to have had
or to have the equanimity to propose that it comes to
the choice of a false reason or none at all.

In whatever event, if one *thinks* about what is the
case and what is not the case seriously, intensely, and
long enough, one seems either to drive oneself insane
or to come to the conclusion that almost everyone else
is or that we all are, when it comes down to it, one
might say, metaphysically.

A few hard-headed Scotsmen (Reid and others—

* Jowett translation.

the philosophers of common sense)* insisted that even if our thinking can lead us up a garden path paved by logical consistency into metaphysical nightmare, spiritual hell, moral nihilism, and a total intellectual débâcle in irresolvable paradoxes, nevertheless they were not abdicating *their* common sense.

However, I am unable to 'believe in', or 'trust', ultimately, my 'common sense', either. I wish I could, but I do not seem to be in control of these matters.

Yet 'behind', as it were, all this sort of thing, I have held for most of my life, and do so now, more than ever, certain—I'm not sure what best to call them— convictions? but authorized by what or whom?

God given? genetically—culturally determined? chosen? and if so, wishfully?

Nevertheless, however much I riddle them with my own riddles and sometimes ridicule, *they* do seem to determine, or at least affect, the direction of my life. I have become convinced of *that,* as an empirical fact, from my observation of both my life and others.

I serve values, not always faithfully or constantly, but I nevertheless feel *bound* to them, I can't get away from them. If I can't prove them right, I can't prove them wrong. They are not contrary to my common sense, though they often run counter to what seem to be my short-term interests, certainly my short-term inclinations.

But not to my long-term inclinations. I want to live correctly. To live correctly cannot be wrong. There *must* be a correct way to live. That way must conform to the nature of life, and to what is the case.

What *is* our environment?

Does what is, what is the case, include spiritual, emotional environments, which are not secondarily, tertiarily, or quaternally derived from our physical environment?

It is no use trying to split up and fragment the

* S. A. Grave, *The Scottish Philosophy of Common Sense,* Oxford University Press, London, 1960.

problem under the pretence that this is *analysing* the problem.

For example. Truth and lying.

In the course of my professional work as well as elsewhere I have come across something like this scenario often. It is so common, typologically, as to dissolve anyone's anxieties that they could be identified by it.

The simple story of sexual infidelity, deceit, jealousy, etc. The secret affair between a man and his wife's best friend. The (sometimes simultaneous) affair between a woman and her husband's best friend, married to her best friend.

If it is decided to follow the path of deception, as things go on, sometimes for years and years, an extraordinarily complex, intricate pattern of misrepresentations, equivocations, and outright lies has to have been woven, and kept up, with some measure of consistency.

Then a lady of seventy discovers that her husband has had a mistress for the last thirty years. That all her friends knew. Those business conferences! and all the usual rest of it. She is maybe jealous. But she is quivering, physically, because she says, and I have no reason to disbelieve her, her *whole sense of reality* has been shattered. Her mind runs through all those years: she discovers she has been shrouded in a tissue of deception, all those years. She is past being outraged. She feels desperate because she has been cheated of reality. She has been deprived of truth. I'm sure that truth deprivation can wreak as much havoc to some people as vitamin deprivation.

We *need* truth. Truth and reality seem sometimes virtually indistinguishable, sometimes separable, but always most intimately related.

What is the case must include my environment, and to live correctly, my genes need to know what is the case.

In the end, what determines in law whether someone

is completely 'gone' or not is the answer to the question: Does he or she know the difference between right and wrong?

After practising 'psychiatry' for twenty-five years, I ought to have been able to come to some at least testable scientific hypotheses. Come across some facts that point in one direction or another.

But the facts seem to be pointable in many directions. They themselves seem largely dependent on us for the type/form of existence we take them to have.

It seems that they themselves cannot be our ultimate authority, since we, if we do not construct them entirely, as some have said, still seem unable not to construe them in some way or other not finally dictated by the facts themselves.

We come back to ourselves as our own final authority. But if we are as far, or as much, as we can appeal to, then many of the shrewdest of our fellows have refused to go farther than to say that though we ourselves are all we have to go on, we may ourselves be so limited and/or even so deranged, that as media for truth, we have not a snowball's chance in hell.

Words attributed to reputed spiritual, religious, intellectual world figures attribute to us, sometimes to themselves as well, gross ignorance, confusion, spiritual darkness, innate moral depravity.

Opinions vary as to whether such is the state of affairs. If it is, is it remediable? If remediable, by human effort or by the grace of God, if there is a God, alone?

In this morass, I feel like a disoriented blind bat sinking into quicksand, without even being able to feel gleeful in the assurance that anyone is in a better position.

yet 'Surely beyond that last blue ridge of mountains rimmed with snow.

     dwells a man who knows why men are born?'

They have been married four years. And have only one child. He has been studying spiritual-mental disciplines of Northern India and Tibet. Is particularly drawn to the tantric world.

He has affairs with other women. In particular, *an* other women, whom he has staying with them.

As his wife enters the sitting room one afternoon there they are on the sofa.

'It's too much! I can't stand it! Get that woman out of the house,' she yelled.

'That's not a woman,' he replied, referring to the object beside him, on the sofa.

'that's a waterfall.'

I don't know whether I've got a problem at all that's what I've come to see you about

to cut a long story short

It's my six-year-old daughter she was doing very badly at school she was behind with her reading and writing and arithmetic and she was insufferable to me wouldn't do anything I asked her I could do nothing with her and then about two months ago butter wouldn't melt in her mouth and suddenly she was reading, and writing, and top in her class in arithmetic I knew something was up and I asked her what had come over her and she said 'Nothing mummy' but I knew she was lying so I got it out of her I couldn't believe it I just couldn't believe it she was having an *affair* with my husband her father she was sucking his penis every other day and they were carrying on like that under my very roof I asked her why she hadn't told me and she said 'I didn't want to upset you mummy' and I can't tell the police because I love him and she would never forgive me and now he's having an affair with her best friend and I think the whole class is starting to queue up what do you think? when I challenged him he just asked me to join them then I thought this is probably what I wanted to do with my father if I had done that with my father I wouldn't be all screwed up like I am now very likely. I wish he had been my daddy. do you think there is a problem?

Moonlight plays on a silver stream in the jungle.

The young man has a commanding presence: gentle, charming, reserved, handsome. His devotees are all Indians. They take him to be Mahavatar Babaji.

A cultured old Indian lady is telling me of her meetings with Babaji, as he sits next to her, inclining his head attentively.

She had met Babaji three times in her life. This third time, she is an old woman and he, the young man we are sitting with. Last time, about thirty years ago, they were both in middle age. And the first time was a long, long time ago, when he was a very old man, and she, a very young girl.

There is a professor of chemistry at Banaras.

He specializes in laser research.

He told me that while pursuing his researches in Japan, an Indian gentleman, dressed in a dhoti, came into his laboratory.

He told the professor to return to Banaras to continue his research. There was no further conversation.

They walked to the door of the laboratory. His visitor put a hand on his shoulder, and disappeared into thin air.

The professor went immediately to his Japanese colleague, with whom he was engaged in research, told him of the visit, and that he would have to wind up his work there and return to India.

This was accepted without demur, and he returned to Banaras where his research continues.

A friend of mine told me he had asked a Tibetan tulku, reputed to be a Bodhisattva, whether or not he believed the stories of a wonder-working Indian guru, who seems to produce sophisticated pieces of matter out of the air.

The Tibetan replied: 'I don't know whether to believe that sort of thing or not.'

My friend was nonplussed, because he thought that someone of the Tibetan's spiritual station *should* know whether to believe 'that sort of thing' or not.

When I told this story to another friend of mine who is as knowledgeable about reputed sages all over the place as anyone I know, he evinced no surprise. 'That's the type of mind they have cultivated.'

In many conversations in India, between cultivated, educated people, it was evident to me that there was a profound (but not that easy to see or express clearly) difference in how we took things to be. For them (allow a reckless generalization) anything was possible. Under usual circumstances, there was a high antecedent probability that certain things would happen, or that they would not. But the conscious beyond consciousness of the holy man is at one with the One and All, wherein *all* possibilities reside. Not just our predictions. Man proposes, God disposes.

A Christian theologian said to me, it's not a question of what God *can* do, it's a question of what he *does* do.

When I was fourteen, I was asked what I wanted to study when I was older. I replied without hesitation: 'Psychology, philosophy, and theology.' I was quickly in disgrace when I would not give more than the foggiest account of what each of these terms meant.

Let us say that psychology is the study of the psyche, philosophy is the love of wisdom, and theology an attempt to articulate the relation of creation to the divine.

Most people called psychologists today probably don't believe that a psyche exists, except as the manifestation of certain physical functions, many present-day philosophers believe that all but a very few of their predecessors were disastrously wrong in their methods and conclusions, and many present-day theologians would be regarded by almost all their predecessors as heretics and/or atheists.

By the time I was seventeen, the philosophers I had read arrived, each more or less convincingly and persuasively, at what seemed incompatible contradictions between them. There was no consensus. Human beings the world over regarded by millions as sages taught diverse doctrines including the doctrine of no doctrine. So in psychology and theology everyone differed. How could us newcomers decide right from wrong, truth from falsity? The very nature of what was a fact was up for grabs.

I abandoned everything else and took to science. Not what science might at any time present us with as, provisionally, fact, but the scientific *method*. Here at least the human mind had arrived at a way of proceeding which, if it perhaps could never solve the riddle of the universe, common sense schooled to the sharpness of sagacity, might reconcile us to the necessary disenchantment at resigning ourselves, more or less gracefully, to our limitations.

However, although I thought I wanted to study embryology, and neurophysiology in particular, I found that I could not keep away from psychoanalysis. From the start, I had grave misgivings as to whether pychoanalysis was a science, since I doubted that it proceeded by a scientific *method*. But my fascination overruled my qualms, and I have found that, despite myself, it has been over matters psychological, philosophical, and theological that my mind has pondered through the years. Often with a most unpleasant sense of the vanity of such pondering.

Let me go back to some words, as an example of the problem I am trying to express.

A strong resonance in the word from which 'to sin' is translated is 'to miss the mark', in archery, to be 'off' target. Even is this is not the only note in the complex chord of this word, it changes for me the quality of the sense of the word I grew up with in my immediate Scottish Presbyterian culture. It aligns the term to such terms as 'error', such expressions as 'to err is human, to forgive divine'.

Kierkegaard made it clear to me that contrition was not what I thought 'guilt' was.

'Give us each day our daily bread.' 'Daily' is a translation of a Greek word, literally meaning 'superessential'.

And so on. Not only the trustworthiness of the most authentic earliest MS is disputed, but the translations therefrom.

To investigate one of any such matters at first hand one has to devote a full lifetime, and even then would not stand a chance of holding an opinion worth having on innumerable issues of complex scholarship without an exceptionally fine intellect and very rare qualities of character.

In every field, the field itself is so vast that to be a good all-rounder in just one speciality deserves respect.

Nevertheless, there is still the fallacy of not being able to see the woods for the trees. Difficult if one is oneself a tree in the woods, not even one of the tallest. Difficult if there is no vantage point outside the woods, from which to survey the woods.

It seems to be incontrovertible that someone said that someone said that he was the way, the truth, and the life. And that in that capacity he promised that whenever two or three people were gathered together in the name of the Way, the Truth, and the Life, there 'I' am in the midst.

Even if we do not know the way or cannot believe that there *is* a way, even if we don't know the truth or don't believe that there is *the* truth, and even if life with a capital L seems mumbo jumbo, if in the name of these matters we still come together, then 'I', which is not the hallucinations we have inside each of our sacks of skin, is in our midst.

That seems to me a most profound proposition.

Dare I believe it? Dare I not?

This book is haunted by the question: What is the correct way to live? When I put this question, through an interpreter, to a reputed saint in Kashmir, said to be over a hundred years old (he looked like an ancient bird), the instant answer, through the interpreter, was:

Let your heart be like the sun
Shine alike on everyone.

Whence did he derive this knowledge? Or was it mere opinion?

'The scientific and technical world of modern man,' writes C. F. von Weizsäcker, 'is the result of his daring enterprise, knowledge without love.' * Chilling. I cannot see how knowledge without love can yield knowledge of love; how a heartless method, yielding heartless results, can do anything else than explain *away* the heart.

Werner Heisenberg, in an address given on the Pnyx hill in Athens in 1964,† after a searching probe into our capacity to 'understand' the world mathematically, suggests that 'patterns in our minds', called archetypes by Plato, may 'reflect the internal structure of the world' in ways mathematics cannot. 'Whatever the explanation of these other [than mathematical] forms of understanding may be, the language of the images, metaphors and similes, is probably the only way to approach the "one" from wider regions.'

'You Scottish theologians,' a Swiss theologian once said to me, 'just tell stories. You do not theologize.' Parables however may be the only way, sometimes.

This book makes no pretensions to be a guide to the perplexed. I am myself perplexed. But I have tried, as best I can, to convey the nature of my perplexity.

---

* *The History of Nature*, University of Chicago Press, Chicago, 1949, p. 190.

† 'Natural Law and the Structure of Matter', The Rebel Press, London, 1970, pp. 44, 45. The English version is by Heisenberg.

Can what is morally wrong be scientifically right? Two worlds shatter each other.

Toward the end of his life, C. G. Jung had the nerve to write: 'We must completely give up the idea of the psyche being somehow connected with the brain . . .' *

I am sure he was not suffering from senile dementia, nor was it a slip of the pen, or an ill-considered statement.

To Lévi-Strauss and many others, Bergson, Sartre, and, I would imagine, Jung are prime examples of 'savage minds' in our twentieth-century civilized midsts. In 1913, Albert Schweitzer undertook a psychiatric study of Jesus, and against the opinion of a number of eminent psychiatrists concluded that there was insufficient evidence to pronounce him insane.

However, he could give him the benefit of the doubt only by discounting much of what he seemed to mean, and by culturally relativizing his world view.

St Catherine of Siena is credited with the remark:
All the way to Heaven
            is Heaven.
For has He not said,
            I am the Way?

* 'Synchronicity', in *The Interpretation of Nature and the Psyche, Pantheon*, New York, 1955, p. 123. I do not quote Jung here because I agree with this statement. I do not understand it, but I respect it.